Telemarketing:
The Keys to Success

Telemarketing:
The Keys to Success

Bernard Caïazzo

translated by Pierre Frottier

INDUSTRIAL
SOCIETY
PRESS

First published in Great Britain, 1991 by
The Industrial Society Press
Robert Hyde House
48 Bryanston Square
London W1H 7LN
Telephone: 071-262-2401

© English language edition, The Industrial Society Press, 1991

Translated by Pierre Frottier

Originally published in France, 1989, by Dunod as *Les Clés du Succès en Télémarketing*

© French edition, Bordas, Paris, 1989

British Library Cataloguing in Publication Data
Caïazzo, Bernard
    Telemarketing: The keys to success.
    I. Title
    658.8

    ISBN 0–85290–811–3

Typeset by Columns Design and Production Services Ltd, Reading
Printed by Billings, Worcester
Cover by PGT Design

CONTENTS

CONTENTS

CONTENTS

FOREWORD

In the beginning, when Bernard Caïazzo adapted Murray Roman's book *How to Build Your Business By Telephone* to the French market by publishing *Telephone Marketing: Prospecter et Vendre Par Telephone*, I never thought this work would sell more than 10,000 copies in France, giving it the highest ever sales of any work on that subject. I also never imagined that this publication would promote the creation of so many companies in the field of telemarketing in France. In the United States, according to the very reliable figures given by ATT, telemarketing is a $50 million plus industry, while development in Europe is considerable.

In view of the wealth of information it contains, this second work by Bernard Caïazzo, which this time is not an adaptation but a complete personal product, should be viewed as the Bible of telemarketing for Europe. It will promote the creation of new telemarketing endeavours and will bring know-how to others.

Bernard Caïazzo has shown great courage in giving away so much advice and in relating so much about the personal experience he has acquired in telemarketing. As far as I am concerned I have never wanted to write such a book. I therefore admire the author, who because of his outstanding experience can be considered the greatest telemarketing specialist in Europe, assuring him of the continued confidence of large companies. It is probable that this work will also sell more than 10,000 copies.

We had the Old Testament from our late master in the commercial use of the telephone, Murray Roman; we now have Bernard Caïazzo's New Testament.

Michael Violanti
President, Phone Marketing America

INTRODUCTION

Outstanding successes in telemarketing

In the United States, 145,000 companies operate an in-house telemarketing service. This is used for direct selling, and for setting up sales appointments, as well as giving information to consumers, and gathering information by phone.

Telemarketing has many uses, and is only limited by our creativity. However, one thing is certain in the United States: if you do not operate a telemarketing system, you will be as powerless as if you had no field sales consultants.

In America the executive in charge of achieving sales objectives will not consider operating without the support of telemarketing. For Americans, telemarketing has become almost a 'run of the mill' part of managing a business.

In France today, the level of telecommunications equipment is now equivalent to that of the United States. As a result, France will see continuing growth in the use of telemarketing, defined as a *'measurable* system of communication between a company and its clients, based on the interactive nature of the telephone'.

In Europe, telemarketing went through its first phase of growth between 1978 and 1985. The objective during the initial phase was that it should achieve credibility with companies. At that time, most companies did not believe in the effectiveness of the telephone as a strategic weapon for their marketing operations, and American multinationals had to convince their European subsidiaries to test out this method with a view to improving the efficiency of their sales operations.

Faced with a reversal of the balance of supply and demand, the exponentially rising costs of face-to-face sales meetings, and problems relating to the processing of small order clients, the objective was to find a means of maintaining a commercial dialogue that would be more cost-effective than selling face-to-face.

The first Europeans to use telemarketing were IBM, Kodak, Rank Xerox, AMEX, 3M . . . and, following successful test operations, telemarketing developed in Europe, initially in the United Kingdom and then in France, the German Federal Republic, Benelux, and more recently in Italy and Spain.

The United Kingdom was the first European country to be convinced, mainly because they spoke the same language as the Americans. This process took place as a result of American specialists setting up in London or through British companies sending their own teams to the United States. Operations started in France about two years later in 1979, when the telemarketing pioneer Murray Roman, at the forefront of telemarketing in the United States, set up an operation in Paris.

Whereas most telemarketing companies in France were attempting to invent their own methods of telemarketing from their early experiences with clients, ten years ago I was lucky enough to have Murray Roman support me in establishing telemarketing in France.

In 1979, as a result of many visits to the United States and with on-site support in Paris from American consultants, we had successfully acquired and adapted skills for this new activity from case studies undertaken for the largest companies in the United States, which were all telemarketing clients of Murray Roman's. Murray Roman invented telemarketing in the United States and in the world. He was the first to understand the extraordinary advantages that marketing could derive from Graham Bell's invention.

The Federal Republic of Germany was next, slightly later than France for two reasons. First, Germany takes longer to integrate new ideas, which in practice often results in their using these ideas more effectively later on. They consider, with good reason, that how something is used is the only thing that counts. Second, German legislation imposes heavy constraints and forbids the phoning of people at home who are not already clients of the company making the phone call.

About the same time, Holland and Belgium followed suit because of their ease of communication with the United States. And finally, first Italy in 1985, then Spain in 1986, started telemarketing operations.

It can be said that in 1988 the United Kingdom, France, Germany and the Benelux countries entered the second phase of telemarketing, which is the most dangerous both for the telemarketing company executive and for you as a potential user.

After the initial creation, there is a period of development which is followed after a few years by the maturity phase.

In the micro computer market, for instance, where a large number of vendors have appeared, the market for telemarketing services has generated the creation of a great number of telemarketing companies. There are now more than 500 companies listed as supplying telemarketing services in France.

The company executive who lacks experience may believe that with telemarketing, as in the printing industry, any company can supply the goods. This is a characteristic feature of the second phase of development of any new activity. It is also one of the main reasons why I decided to write this book: to give the users of telemarketing services the keys to success before they enter this area of activity (which must be considered more than a trade).

What I am most proud of is not that I initiated telemarketing in France and established the first telemarketing services network in Europe; nor that I integrated this activity in-house at IBM, Peugeot, the BNP bank, and in more than a hundred of the top French groups, and it is not that I have received more telemarketing awards than all the other companies put together; it is that I have managed to set up a subsidiary in the United States which is a consultant to AT & T, the American telephone company which is the equivalent of British Telecom. After Murray Roman's death in 1984, I bought out his shareholding, and it has become a 100 per cent French company. I can say that in the field of telemarketing it is a French company which advises the leading American telecommunications company.

The American market is today in the third stage of development, the maturity phase. It is in this stage that the best telemarketing service companies have acquired the in-depth knowledge of the elements necessary to create results.

My objective in publishing this book is to help Europe achieve this stage of maturity as soon as possible. Currently, notable failures are hindering the development of telemarketing, and these are usually the result of poor workmanship.

In the United Kingdom, telemarketing is still in a stage of development where often it is compared to door-to-door selling. British Telecom, however, have a telemarketing services subsidiary. This subsidiary, which is the market leader in the country, and which is managed by a follower of Murray Roman, has endeavoured to get UK companies to understand the importance, in the presence of so many self-styled specialists, of selecting the right partner when deciding to use telemarketing. In spite of this, British Telecom has not succeeded in dispelling this 'door-to-door selling' image which is a product of the misuse of telemarketing.

This book should enable people to avoid making some expensive mistakes. However, it must be kept in mind that success depends upon having defined the problem clearly. The question asked of a company offering telemarketing services must never be, 'What is the cost of 10,000 phone calls?'; the most important question is 'How can telemarketing improve my sales results?'. This question should be addressed with thought, not with the raw mechanics, which is why the consultancy aspect is important in telemarketing. Experience is what counts, so the level of maturity of whoever you choose will determine your level of success.

In the words 'telephone marketing', the operative word is not telephone, but *marketing*. A good telemarketing specialist is first and foremost an excellent marketing specialist in your particular area of activity. If the person you are using does not know your markets your chances of success with telemarketing are reduced by 90 per cent.

Another basic piece of advice is that you should not confuse telemarketing with data processing; the data processing technical expert will seldom turn out to be a telemarketing specialist. Americans express the different approaches as 'high tech' and 'high touch'.

Technology is only one of the tools of telemarketing, so do not be mesmerised by a team of phoners sitting in front of a VDU on which a script is displayed, entering data in real time. Once again it is *thought* which has produced the script, selected and trained the phoners to obtain quality, devised the strategy of approach, oriented accurate targeting, devised the software, developed the programme – it is thought that makes the difference.

When I was visiting the number one American telemarketing services company, the American Trans Tech Company, in Jacksonville, Florida, I found, while standing among phoners operating VDUs within the highly ergonomic environment, that most phoners had an item of personal significance (a child's drawing, a Disneyworld photo, football calendars, etc.) in their work area, which suggested to me that the psychological factor is, in fact, more important than technology.

Another illustration of the importance of the psychological

elements is that the hottest prospect interested in your product has little value if nobody goes to see them. Given that telemarketing is relatively new, your sales force must be made aware of the importance of following up the contacts generated from telemarketing. It is vital that the Account Manager within your chosen telemarketing company creates this awareness in your team.

The three most important points to remember in order to enhance your telemarketing results are:

- the psychology of human relationships
- an in-depth knowledge of marketing
- an appropriate technology.

PART I

STRATEGIES FOR SUCCESS IN BUSINESS

1

THE TELEPHONE AND THE OFFICE EQUIPMENT INDUSTRY

Making appointments

Your objective is to have the potential client or 'prospect' accept a visit from a sales consultant. Every sales expert will tell you that if an appointment has been accepted, you are half way there. The technique for setting up appointments should be well thought out, as it must satisfy two conflicting requirements:

- obtain an appointment without having given so much information that the freshness of the forthcoming presentation of the product will be impaired; but
- give enough information to the client to interest him/her sufficiently to agree to a meeting. Remember:
  - 'The product is the trap.'
  - 'The product is the enemy.'

Those are the principles governing appointment setting operations.

Arranging an appointment develops through five stages.

- Attract the prospective client's attention: make it easy for them to listen to you.
- Arouse interest: they must be interested in hearing you talk about your product.
- Ask questions in order to discover their needs.
- Explain the benefits your product offers to meet that need.
- Set up the appointment.

The first thirty seconds following the first step are vital, and will determine the successful outcome of the call. This means the approach must be very carefully chosen to attract the prospect's interest. There are five main approaches to that end:

- Refer to a common acquaintance.
- Ask a question referring to a mailing.
- Ask a question concerning knowledge of the product.
- Ask a question concerning a new product.
- Refer to a piece of information about the prospect's company which may for instance have been published in the media.

It is very important to talk about *benefits* and not only about *characteristics*. This means that instead of saying 'This telephone has touch dialling', it is better to say 'Because this telephone has touch dialling, you will save time'.

Any characteristic of your product stays the same whoever uses it; the *benefit* is specific to the user. When communicating benefits on the phone, personalise them by referring to the prospect directly: 'your company', 'to help you', 'your costs'. . . .

More and more companies have a pool of phoners who specialise in setting up appointments for the sales team. There are two main orders of reason for this, psychological and financial.

Psychological reasons

Sales people prefer face-to-face contact to telephone conversations, and prefer to get the feel of the client in their own working environment. A visit allows the best possible perception of the client's attitudes and environment: the way an office is decorated, a simple facial expression, a secretary's intervention, will reveal important information not provided by the telephone. These elements are reference points without which the sales person feels ill at ease.

Face-to-face selling is a specialised job. It is essential for the sales person to have a relationship of trust with the specialist phoner who sets up their appointments.

Financial reasons

When the sales team are setting up appointments on the phone, they are not out on visits and are not selling. If someone else is making appointments for them, they have more time in the field making sales. Also, a specialist in appointment setting costs less than a sales person, which is also a saving for the company. A sales person's time costs, in general, three or four times more than a professional phoner's time. For example, a phoner receives £833.33 per month when employed full time (£416.66 on half-time) which represents a cost to the company of £1,250 including National Insurance, etc. A sales person is paid £1,250 per month full time as a fixed salary which costs £1,875 to the company.

If appointment setting produces one appointment per hour, the cost of appointment setting is 50 per cent higher if the sales person is setting up his/her own appointments. Therefore I recommend that one full-time phoner should set appointments for two field sales people working full-time. This pattern has worked successfully elsewhere.

The phoner can usually manage to set up eight appointments during a full working day, giving the two sales people four visits each. If the sales person cannot attend four visits per day, you could have one phoner to four sales people, or, if the number of appointments that your sales people can attend is high, two phoners for three sales people.

The phoner, operating full-time, brings in this way a number of benefits to the sales person:

- They improve the relationship with the client; the phoner can play the part of an assistant.
- Any appointments made will be well-qualified as the phoner is a specialist, as opposed to the sales person who may not like the telephone as a means of communication.
- The phoner will be able to give clients an immediate response to any queries if the sales person is absent or out in the field.
- The phoner can assist the sales person in their administrative tasks and be a great help to the sales manager.

Phoners can also be useful in communicating information between the other members of the team. They will have general information about clients which will be of use in case the sales person is not available. Companies like IBM in the data processing industry and Canon in the photocopying industry use this relationship of phoner and sales person with great success. It is extremely likely that these methods will eventually be applied by all companies selling equipment goods.

It must be stressed that the success of this activity is largely down to smooth coordination and clear communication between phoner and sales person. The sales person must inform the phoner about the results of the appointment. The phoner should highlight the best contacts and let the sales person know about 'hot' opportunities. Without this relationship, this method or system will only be half as effective. It is therefore a good idea to give the phoner bonuses or incentives relating to the results obtained by the sales team, without making things too complicated to manage.

Arranging a meeting at the sales person's office

This type of contact is different from the usual type of appointment because of the difficulty there is in getting the potential client to make the visit. The reason such a visit may be necessary is to give a demonstration of the product (cars, computers, video systems, etc.). The client has to be highly motivated to agree to make the visit and often will have shown this by sending back a coupon, or responding to information in the media or to a mailshot. It may be the technical originality of a new product which is the successful trigger. As a general rule, the telephone is five or ten times more effective than a mailshot on its own. Companies such as Kodak or Nashua have successfully used such methods for the launching of a new range of products. Service companies in the data processing industry in America use this technique extensively.

Of course, if a client is unavailable to attend a demonstration on a particular day, you can use this opportunity to arrange a meeting at their office. This method is best in those cases where the client really needs to have *seen* a sophisticated piece of equipment operating before being able to make a decision.

A confirmation call has to be made to the client a few hours before he/she is due to arrive to ensure that all the necessary instructions on how to get there, where to park, etc., have been given.

In the same way, inviting a group of potential clients to attend an event concerning their area of interest, or to get better acquainted with a new product, is an excellent way of using telemarketing. Here, the telephone is essential to ensure the success of the event. You can discuss clients' expectations and let them know who else will be there. Often, the topic of such an event may not be particularly attractive to the potential customer, but they will come because a well-known personality had said they would be there.

One piece of advice is do not send invitations before making phone calls to inform the customer of the event and answer any questions (remember – 'the product is the trap'). It is very important to call the customer once the invitation has been received to confirm his/her attendance. A final confirmation call 48 hours before the event will ensure their attendance and demonstrate your reliability. For example, I once called back customers who had received an invitation from the organisers of an office-automation exhibition. Less than 1 per cent of the people invited had sent back their acceptance card; 350 *extra* acceptances were obtained after 1,000 phone calls.

You can improve attendance by taking into account where your customers live and work when organising events. The proximity of the event to the customer's home is especially important for events such as breakfast presentations: reduce the distance the customer has to travel and your rate of attendance will improve.

This method, of companies offering services to businesses for instance, will give significantly better results than other methods (visits from field sales teams, mailings, etc.). In addition to this the cost of such an event can be reduced as guests will pay a fee for attending the event. You can further increase the effectiveness of these events by having a low ratio of customers to sales people; four customers to each sales person is the maximum.

Surveys, information gathering and research

The telephone does not only have to be used to sell products or set up appointments. Telephoning allows you to gather information. The information gathered is extremely useful to your company and can inform your sales staff. The calls are an important part of marketing and will reveal the needs of the market.

When we consider the needs of a market, it is usually the total needs which are referred to: a product 'X' fulfils the needs of a market in general; this does not mean that all consumers will buy it. Telephone marketing enables you to define not only the global needs of a market, but the special needs of each client separately. A 'pre-launch survey' will allow you to know these needs more precisely, and is the best way to select a target population according to what they want. A pre-launch survey is the selection, sorting and qualification of customers through screening using the terminology appropriate to each area of activity.

Systematic research must neither be too lengthy nor too qualitative in its approach as telephone interviews could turn out to be costly.

Experience shows that by using multiple choice questions it is possible to find out in great detail on the telephone what the potential client's expectations and habits are. Using this data, it is easier to guide your sales team towards the best opportunities the market offers.

You may have doubts about obtaining answers from the people you contact. In all the pre-selling surveys I have carried out, I have never found more than 10 per cent refuse to answer.

You should not ask direct questions during the opening phase of the telephone conversation; it is better to put 'closed' questions, offering the prospect a choice of answers concerning general views, and then gradually get to direct questions concerning the customer's company.

Remember that during pre-selling telephone interviews, information about companies which have no short-term needs is also of great value. In the medium- or long-term this information will allow better timing for re-contacting these companies.

Example

A pre-selling survey was conducted for a company offering consultancy in data processing. The targeted companies were separated into groups: 200 to 500 employees; 500 to 2,000 employees; more than 2,000 employees. The objective was to get to know the habits and needs of these companies. Analysis of the answers enabled the consultancy company to devise a strategy of approach. Appointments were made following a second telephone call to the potential client.

As a result of this survey, 13 per cent of the companies interviewed expressed a wish to meet a sales person and 7 per cent eventually contracted for some research work. Taking into account the fact that all contracts represented a sale of between £10,000 and £50,000, it is easy to see how cost-effective this method can be.

Information supplied to the sales people enables them to organise an agenda of contacts to be made and to act at the right time. Certain companies in the photocopying industry carry out systematic surveys of other companies to establish their current and future needs in photocopying machines. These surveys collect information concerning the size of the company, the impact of a competitor product, needs for new equipment, and, in particular, make it possible to take advantage of short-term opportunities to deploy the sales team most efficiently.

These surveys can often be the occasion to set up appointments, if a company has an immediate need. These appointments give particularly good results if a prospect has expressed a specific need. This system can offer cost efficiency in addition to psychological well-being (no depressing visits!). Survey interviews can also be recorded and the sales person can listen to the tape *en route* to the appointment, thereby getting a feel for the client's attitude.

It has long been considered that a good sales person could always sell, even to somebody who had reservations. Even if this is true – although I do not know any sales person who achieves 100 per cent sales rate – this view is not positive from the client's point of view. Your objective must not be to get clients to sign an order they will later regret, as in the long-term a buyer who is not satisfied with his/her decision to buy is bad business for your company. A sales person who forces orders is not an asset to your company.

I believe that in future years most companies, particularly those selling equipment, will carry out systematic pre-selling surveys to supply their sales people with a high-volume of good quality leads. For this to be possible, the level of gross profit per sale must be sufficient to cover the cost of such surveys.

Direct selling of supplies

In the field of office technology, clients are big users of consumable supplies and development products, and there has been an extraordinary development in the area in the last few years. Earlier, suppliers of data processing equipment would give their clients a telephone number to place their orders for consumables as they required them. This is the passive approach to selling. Suppliers of hardware then realised the kind of profit margin competitors were getting selling consumables for their machines, so they set up telemarketing teams themselves to make outgoing calls to take orders.

Selling consumables is no longer considered a secondary activity in the office technology industry. While it is true that value of sales in the consumables department of a hardware supplier are six to eight times lower than the hardware sales the profit margin may be greater for the consumables.

Companies in the data processing hardware industry therefore organised themselves for selling consumables on the telephone both through out-going and in-coming calling. It is now common-place for telesales in this area to produce sales reaching £10,000, including small machines such as VDU stations or printers.

The fourth level of telesales for office equipment supplies addresses existing as well as potential clients. You need the support of a good catalogue and a genuine intention to ensure a wide circulation to capture a market share among potential customers who are not already hardware clients.

This approach has enabled some companies to double their sales. However, it needs a very professional telesales operation which will include at least fifteen phoners to cover a country such as Great Britain.

The cost-effectiveness of this approach relies on five issues:

- Selecting and training a supervisor who brings a professional approach to the telephoning environment. Success depends on having a motivated team, which largely depends on the supervisor.
- Being equipped to make both in-coming and out-going calls.
- Monitoring the productivity of the calls made by the team.
- Creativity in the script-writing so that your team uses original approaches.
- The support of an experienced telesales services company, so that over time all aspects of the operation remain up-to-date and relevant.

Computerisation is indispensable if you are to improve productivity and to ensure the correct timing of calls to each client. Having analysed clients' ordering profiles, and having data-processed and stored the information, daily actions can be programmed to contact clients whose orders have not been received at the expected time.

Telesales people must work in real time with the VDU operators so that they can access all the necessary information concerning the clients' order renewals, stocks, special prices for particular clients, etc.

2

THE TELEPHONE AND THE CAR INDUSTRY

A case history: Ford, 1962

In 1962, the marketing executives at Ford decided to test out the effectiveness of telephoning techniques by running a sales programme to supply Ford dealers with leads. They did this with the support of the J. Walter Thompson advertising agency and the Communicator Network Inc. (CNI).

Some 15,000 housewives were recruited and trained to make telephone calls from their homes. With little or no previous selling experience and no special selling skills, these women managed to obtain an average of two 'hot' leads per day for each of Ford's 23,000 dealers. Using a carefully devised script, these women made contact with twenty million homes at the rate of one million calls per week, to find out whether the people contacted were potential car buyers and, if so, within what period they were going to buy. The questions they asked were as follows:

1 Do you, or does anybody in your home, intend to buy a car within the next two years? (If not, close the conversation with a 'Thank you'.)
2 When do you expect to buy? In the next three months, six months, a year?
3 Will you be buying a new or second-hand car?
4 Will it be a large or small car?
5 Do you own a car already or is there anybody in your home who owns a car? (If no, go to Question 8.)
6 Can you tell me the make and year of origin of the car you have?
7 Did you buy it new or second-hand?
  (They only asked Question 8 in the cities where there were several post codes.)

8   Can you tell me what your post code is?
    (If asked why they replied 'To help me find the Ford dealer
    who is the closest to your home. We can then send him your
    name so he can contact you and tell you about his cars'.)
    (They ended the call with: 'Thank you very much for your
    cooperation.')

The simplicity of this well-structured script kept the time
required for each call to an absolute minimum and the phoner was
also in a position to give the Ford dealer the names and particulars
of the best potential customers on the same day as the call was
made. The names of people who had expressed an intention to
buy a car within three months were on the sales person's list
within 24 hours!

The names of people intending to buy a car in six months' time
were sent by mail to the Ford division the day after the call, and a
series of mailshots were made in the intervening period to help
set up a sales appointment. People intending to buy after a period
of two years were followed up carefully, being sent special
brochures and mailshots.

So, what was the result of these efforts?

• Telephone calls detected 340,000 people intending to buy a
  car in the near future; of these, 187,000 turned out to be
  ready to buy a car within the next three months.

• The first day that it became possible to measure the results, it
  was shown that the number of sales recorded was 440 cars;
  nine days later the figure had increased to 7,773.

• The whole programme generated sales for the Ford division at
  an overall cost per sale which was considerably lower than that
  of other promotional methods.

• It is also important to know that whereas 40 per cent of the
  'hot' contacts detected during the telephone campaign were
  current owners of Ford automobiles, the other 60 per cent
  were owners of competitor makes.

When assessing the value of the telemarketing project, 75 per
cent of Ford dealers who had participated considered it *excellent*,
adding comments such as 'one of the best' and 'the best
programme the division ever carried out'. The enthusiasm of the
dealers and the commitment of the sales people, led marketing
executives to state that the programme showed 'all the features of
a successful marketing campaign' – demonstrating the cost-
effectiveness of such a project.

Using the telephone to secure client loyalty

In Europe, the telephone has become one of the main means of communication to increase client loyalty to a car manufacturer. In the struggle to gain a market share, those who win will be the manufacturers who keep in regular touch with their clients from the date of acquisition. This can be done on a computer which enables clients to be contacted regularly through a series of mailshots and phone calls, for example along the following lines:

1 One month after the car was bought, send out a survey to find out the level of satisfaction among purchasers.
2 One year later: send out a 'Happy birthday to the car' mailshot.
3 Two years later: a 'Second anniversary' mailshot.
4 After 27 months find out if the owner is in the market for a new car, and then set an appointment for a test drive.
5 After 36 months: repeat 4.

While mailshots can be organised by computer, the telephone calls require personal contact.

Securing client loyalty on the phone involves employing a sales person who is thoroughly trained and has excellent organisation skills. All car dealers should be capable of telephoning to secure client loyalty once they have been fully trained and have been supplied with a script which will have been carefully prepared and tested by telephone communication experts. Organising the sales person's calls properly should mean they still have time to carry out their other duties efficiently.

A sales person who makes fifteen sales a month should contact each client three times, which means 45 contacts each month, which will not require more than 69 hours of telephone work per month, ie. less than half an hour a day. In large dealerships and branches, it is possible to use professional phoners to make these calls.

It is usually more efficient and cost-effective to employ professional phoners rather than sales people who cannot give all their time to telephoning. Phoners should work in close contact with the sales team as this will create better coordination.

Using the telephone to acquire new clients

Acquiring new clients has become increasingly important in a highly competitive market. In France, the market for cars cannot absorb all of the private cars being built or imported into the country, and 10 per cent of the cars will stay unsold. Companies in the car industry who know how to activate their distribution by using the most modern techniques will be the only survivors. The telephone is an essential tool for establishing new contacts.

In the process of securing client loyalty, the telephone is the most essential means for detecting clients' buying intentions and is far more efficient than mailing. The telephone allows you to detect buying intentions within different time scales, three months, six months, a year and to segment targets into four categories:

- Very 'hot' contacts to be visited urgently.
- Potential customers to be visited within two to three months.
- 'Warm' prospects to visit in six months to a year's time.
- 'Cold' prospects to be followed up after a year.

3

THE TELEPHONE AND HOME OWNERS

Out-going calls and prospecting

The telephone is the ideal means to find out the buying intentions of a target population systematically because it enables you to screen whole lists in a short time.

However, it is neither possible nor cost-effective to contact a whole country's population. The only solution is to select your target to obtain the most effective lists. Ninety per cent of buyers will share certain psychographic criteria (age, income, position, etc.). The list you want can be specified by going to specialist list brokers, or by means of campaigns of games, or by analysing your own client population.

This last method is useful because all you need to do is rank your own client list to determine the basic criteria corresponding to the profile of your future clients. By using the geographical location of your past clients, you can find your future clients. By running a survey on that whole area, you can determine potential buyers' addresses. Your sales force finds the addresses you are interested in in that particular location. Once that list is drawn up, systematic telephoning can start.

The key to successfully locating interested people is the rate at which telephone contacts are made. On average 5 to 10 per cent of telephone contacts are potential purchasers. Obviously, the more people you phone the greater the number of potential customers you will contact.

In general, twenty contacts results in one useful one. These twenty contacts must be made as quickly as possible. If it turns out that someone is not interested, waste no time on the phone but move on to the next one. As it is possible to make twenty contacts every hour, you should be making one really useful contact per hour.

One sale can usually be made as a result of approximately fifteen useful contacts. If the cost of the one useful contact made in each hour of phoning is £31.25, the cost of one sale will be between £312.50 and £468, which with house sales is very reasonable. To obtain this kind of result, you must have good lists, but the involvement of your sales force is the essential element for success: sales people following up telephone contacts must be aware of the efficiency of the system.

In-coming calls

Another way to make good contacts is to include a freephone number in your advertising.

In-coming calls are extremely cost-effective when used in conjunction with radio, newspaper, poster and TV campaigns. You can also advertise your freephone number on television. This is a very immediate way of establishing a link with your company, as the phone is always closer to potential customers than an exhibition centre. About 30 to 35 per cent of people who call a freephone number are genuinely interested in buying your product.

During a call, all the details about the caller must be recorded. It is also important to ask specific questions which enable you to judge a contact's real interest (age, position, income, etc.). Too many companies make the mistake when receiving an in-coming call of not taking down basic information (name, address, etc.) and of not using the opportunity to send out some leaflets. It is a waste not to follow up contacts made at the initiative of the potential customer.

The team of phoners taking in-coming calls must be well trained and work with a script to ensure that as much information as possible is collected. Sales people will then be in a position to follow up the most interesting contacts, and avoid those not fulfilling the criteria.

In the future, it is probable that many adverts will include a freephone number. The aim is for a company to be identified with a freephone number.

Example
October 1983: calling customers after a mailshot.
Potential customers who had been sent some information leaflets were

called back: poor results due to non-targeted list.

A *campaign of phoning the target list in order to find out their buying intention over the two years.*

Seven per cent of people contacted had a genuine intention to buy and sales people followed up systematically with appointments.

The Area Management, who had initiated the sales drive, won the inter-area challenge.

June 1984: 'out-going calling campaign carried out from a list of addresses supplied by the builder'.

People who lived in a geographical area under development were called.

Of the people contacted, 2.6 per cent said they intended to buy a house within six months ('hot' prospects), while 12 per cent had buying intentions within the next two years (warm prospects). The cost per hot prospect was £62.50, and the cost of the telephone campaign per sale was £250 within three months.

March 1985: 'out-going calling of addresses supplied by the builder'.

A teleprospecting team was established within the commercial structure of the builder. Three months after this was set up, phoners had obtained an average of one useful buyer per hour of phoning. The cost of the telephone operation per sale was £416.66.

February 1986: 'campaign following a TV spot'.

A TV advert with a freephone number was shown 36 times between 7 pm and 8 pm during three weeks.

Six thousand calls were received on the freephone number, of which 1,500 were useful calls. This generated 850 visits for the sales people, and resulted in 107 sales. The cost of the whole campaign was £54,166.66, and the cost per house sold was less than £520.83.

Example

January 1987: 'Setting up an in-coming–out-going phoning operation for telemarketing in the centralised national office'.

A team of 30 people capable of processing 400,000 calls per year was set up at a centralised site and given two objectives:

- *to scan through out-going calling lists selected by the regional branches following the requirements laid out by the branches with internal cost allocation; and*
- *to receive in-coming calls rising out of national TV campaigns, processing the callers and transmitting the leads to the local branches.*

In each local branch, a specially trained phoner followed up each contact supplied by the centralised telemarketing operation before it was handed to the sales team. Out of 10,000 weekly calls, 1,000 potential customers were obtained, 100 opportunities followed through, generating ten sales, at a cost of £833.33 per sale. This method proved to be the most successful one.

Conditions for success

These case studies show that the keys to successful telemarketing of houses are:

- a good quality list
- total involvement of the sales team
- coordination of area branches with the main supplier.

4

THE TELEPHONE AND INDUSTRY

Identifying potential customers or 'prospects'

In order to be effective, any sales effort has to be addressed to decision-makers. In a company, especially a larger one, there may be several decision-makers.

In small- and medium-sized companies the decision-maker is easy to find; it is usually the Managing Director. In larger companies, which are usually organised in several departments, the decision-makers become more and more difficult to find.

Everyone knows the story of the sales person who called for ten years on the same department in a large company to get an order, without being aware of the fact that there was another department in the same company on the same floor which used the same products.

Too often the sales person associates only one person with a company. However, it may be possible to sell your product in several divisions of a company, so several people may be involved in the decision-making process. Use the telephone to determine areas of responsibility. Who decides the purchase of a new heavy goods vehicle? The Chief Executive Officer, the Production Director, the Fleet Manager, the drivers?

Finding possible customers

Making an appointment is not the most important objective; identifying a need is more important as it will produce a worthwhile appointment. A telephone marketing operation is divided into four levels of results:

A   People who express a need for your product who accept an appointment.
B   People who express a need for your product who refuse an appointment.
C   People who do not express an interest and who accept an appointment.
D   People who do not express an interest and who refuse an appointment.

Group D is of no interest, and should have no time wasted on it.

Between groups B and C, group B is the more interesting, because the contacts have expressed a need for the product or service offered. It is true that they have not accepted an appointment, but this is only a technical matter which can be solved by a good sales person who can approach the company at another level if necessary to obtain an appointment.

You should not waste your time going to see someone who, even though they have agreed to see you, have not expressed a need for nor an intention to buy your product.

Obviously, companies should not simply make appointments at all costs. It is essential to classify contacts into three categories:

- 'hot' prospects to be met as soon as possible
- 'lukewarm' prospects to be met in six months
- 'cold' prospects to be contacted on the phone in more than six months.

The telephone should be used to sweep the same target regularly and systematically. This will allow 'hot' contacts to be identified. A 'cold' contact could become productive in a year's time.

Example
A large industrial vehicle manufacturer had set up a customer detection operation in order to gain new clients. The objective was systematically to identify prospective buyers over the telephone. Every month the dealers received the names of 50, 100 or 150 potential customers, according to their contract. Overall 100,000 names were viable and 15 per cent of those became 'hot' prospects, resulting in 15,000 buyers.

The Phone Data System

Principle

The Phone Data System is a prospecting system (ie. customer identification) which is based on the link between the telephone and the computer. This system rationalises and optimises client prospecting. This is not a one-off process; it organises an effective prospecting calendar over time. It allows the sales force permanent identification of the best prospects. Telemarketing software is used on-screen and printers send follow-up letters.

Objectives

This system has multiple goals:

- to build the best database possible.
- to develop a more rational and more effective prospecting system.
- to reduce prospecting costs.
- to ensure optimal market coverage.
- to generate the best contacts for the sales force in order to boost sales.

Methodology

The first step is to 'screen', ie. qualify and eliminate, potential prospects. It is essential to work from a list of potential clients.

If a central database does not already exist, use directories, comparative lists, commercial databases or information provided by the sales force, to compile one on the computer. A professional phone team then calls the whole targeted market. The objective is to identify the habits, the needs and the buying potential of each target.

Results

Using the photocopying industry as an example, you need to find out the following:

- monthly consumption of photocopies
- how is the competition positioned
- cost per copy
- what is the potential for converting this prospect into a client?

In the computer industry, you need to know:

- the installed base system
- cost of the systems

- relationships with competitors
- accurate short- and medium-term requirements.

In the industrial machinery field, you need to find out:

- the position of the buyer
- whether it is a second or a third replacement machine
- previous interest shown for your make.

Phoners work on-line, in real time, and with customised software. This on-line system presents numerous advantages:

- The information is immediately captured which means there should be no losses.
- A list of prospects to be called back is automatically brought up by the computer at the beginning of each phoning day.
- The field sales force has access to the computer and can work without any delay or interruptions.
- Each phoner can make between 50 and 100 calls per four hour shift.
- A team of six phoners coached by one supervisor can manage 50,000 contacts per year, working half-time.

This system increases sales productivity in the following ways:

- by increasing the number of productive visits made by the sales team
- by targeting promotional activities onto genuinely potential customers
- by directing efforts on pre-selected visits.

Thanks to the Phone Data System, the sales person can cut the number of visits he/she makes before getting an order by a third.

This system, thanks to the information feedback, allows information to be stored which will be used in the medium-term.

Records are continuously up-dated by the telephoners and, as a result, the sales force possesses a more and more valuable tool. For instance, on a target of 50,000 prospects, the telephone will be able to identify the 5,000 or 6,000 prospects which have the highest sales potential. Instead of going to ten appointments in order to make a sale, the sales person will get a conversion rate in excess of 30 per cent. Furthermore, he/she will be able to plan time spent converting 'lukewarm' prospects into 'hot' prospects. These 'lukewarm' prospects can then be sent mailshots in order to convert them into 'hot' prospects.

Consequences

The database is up-dated every day from information obtained by the phoners. This is a dynamic database which allows selection of prospects according to their level of relevance. The next step is to define the follow-up techniques to develop these prospects, by:

- mailing
- invitation to exhibitions
- specific promotional actions.

Client follow-up

In a replacement market, where each client uses a piece of equipment for several years and then has to replace it, it is essential to keep in contact with each existing customer. When a company's relationship is with distributors or regular purchasing clients, client contact is on-going and, as a result, the sales force knows how to maintain this important link.

In the industrial equipment industry, you must maintain a relationship between sales over several years. This service is best managed by computer. This allows alternate mailings and telephone calls to be conducted by the supplier company.

1 One month after the purchase of the equipment: Customer satisfaction enquiry.
2 One year later: 'first anniversary'.
3 Two years later: 'second anniversary'.
4 Three years later: 'third anniversary'. Include an information leaflet describing the technical progress of the product. Follow up with a telephone enquiry about buying plans.
5 Four years later: Telephone enquiry about purchasing plans to forecast possible replacement.

This method allows for a maximum loyalty response.

You can also use a relatively new technique: the telemessage. The phoner introduces the conversation then asks the client to listen to a specially designed message. This pre-recorded message lasts about 60 seconds. At the end of the telemessage the phoner resumes the conversation.

The telemessage creates a strong credibility and has a very good impact because each word, expression and intonation of the message is designed for maximum effect. You could consider using a popular personality's voice to increase customer loyalty. However, you can also use people who hold relevant senior positions in your company.

Direct sales

Within a client target, taking orders for commonly bought products directly on the phone gives excellent results. Indeed, in combination with sending a catalogue to the client, it is possible, in cases where a visit from the sales person is not cost-effective, to take orders directly on the telephone. (The sales person receives commission on telephone sales.)

However, this system of direct selling must have been agreed by the client, especially when you switch from a sales appointment to a telephone service.

Initially, contact the target asking him or her to take part in a new telephone service which will allow them to order more quickly and more simply. Emphasise the benefits of this system. Up to 90 per cent of clients contacted usually accept this new service since it can only benefit them. Having acquired these clients, it is then simple to implement a regular calling schedule to contact them just prior to stock renewal. This service is very cost-effective since a telephone call is ten to fifteen times cheaper than a sales call.

This system of direct selling on the telephone must not replace sales calls altogether. It will reduce the number of visits and the time saved can be used more effectively on more important clients or for prospecting new clients.

I believe that catalogue selling, both in-coming and out-going, is going to increase considerably in industry.

Example
I set up this direct selling by catalogue system for an office equipment company. This was successful because 85 per cent of clients contacted were willing to order consumables directly on the telephone. Sales people continued to visit the same clients but concentrated their efforts on products with higher margins. This increased the cost-effectiveness of their activity.

5

THE TELEPHONE AND THE BANKING SERVICES INDUSTRY

Integrated phoning and marketing in the banking services industry

In only five years, Citibank became the largest user of telemarketing in the United States. In Britain, telemarketing has a very promising future in the banking sector. Indeed the list of banking products promoted successfully by telemarketing is very long. The number of chequeing accounts, savings accounts, loans and mortgages, pension funds, credit cards, deposit certificates, saving schemes and a whole range of other products increases continually.

Within a competitive environment, where visual solicitation is one of the main obstacles to customer loyalty, the opportunity to speak directly to your target is a privileged way to develop your market. The telephone call establishes this essential link between the bank and a given prospect. However, careful fine-tuning and professionalism is essential for this contact, and the calls should be based on well-structured and pre-tested scripts, and should be made by professional phoners. Do not forget that telemarketing does not function in a void. It is a complement to direct advertising. The telephone increases 2.5 to 10 times the response rate obtained by mailing alone. When the objective is to promote continued relations with clients, these increased ratios can result in considerable short- and long-term benefits.

The telephone adds several important aspects to the global media plan, as follows.

It attracts attention

The direct character of this contact makes people concentrate their attention on the offer being made. If the product offered presents true benefits, the person contacted will be pleased to listen and consider the offer. The willingness of people to participate in telemarketing has often been demonstrated.

It offers immediate in-depth results

A telephone call generates an immediate response. This is important since it allows one to 'work out' the offer before the beginning of the campaign. Tests continue during the preparation cycle. These give feedback on the effect of price changes, conditions, descriptions and target markets.

It adapts the offer

Starting from a first offer, which does not always correspond to the needs of the prospect, it is possible to promote other bank products that are more adapted to the prospect's needs.

Cross-selling: a high potential area

In order to make best use of the telephone, banks should concentrate their efforts towards cross-selling rather than prospecting for new clients.

The best results obtained through telemarketing come from people who already know the organisation which is calling them. Clients who already have accounts in a bank have indicated their goodwill and initiated a continuous relationship. The telephone contact is built around that relationship and encourages the individual called to direct their demand for other financial services towards the same source.

Telemarketing is the most effective way to sell a group of services and increase significantly sales of services per client. This marketing strategy is particularly cost-effective since a single, well-structured campaign can sell several products during a single call.

Telemarketing campaigns give results in cross-sales of new accounts, credit cards, cash cards, automatic savings account, chequeing accounts, cheques, savings accounts and banking services. Cross-selling of all services has a great potential. Another area where the telephone presents exceptional results is in the field of soliciting deposits. A campaign encouraging clients to convert their deposit certificates when they reach maturity gives excellent results. Too many banks handle mature saving bonds by sending a standard mailing, and ignore the potential of tele-marketing.

Other successful cross-selling applications include:

- identification of potential clients needing loans and re-mortgages
- sales of credit cards to consumers and companies.

A case study

In 1977, a large bank in America decided to introduce an automatic service to pay bills through the telephone. This service was then practically unknown to the public. This service, called the 'Billing System', was offered free to new subscribers during the first six months. The campaign started with a press conference explaining the details of the system; there were demonstrations of the 'Billing System' for clients in their local branches, there were adverts on television and in the press, and there were mailings. In order to coordinate these efforts there was also a telephone marketing campaign.

There was no problem in building an appropriate list of contacts. The bank's computer classified the client list in different groups depending on the services they used.

The test sample was a group of clients which was selected according to whether they used automatic cash withdrawal machines or credit cards issued by the bank. Several days before being called, each client received a letter describing the 'Billing System'. The phoners asked the prospects if they had received the letter, and asked if they would be prepared to listen to a brief recorded message by the bank's President explaining the offer.

The use of a recorded message by a senior person had much more impact than the description of the service alone. It showed the seriousness of the offer, and helped to convince people to listen to the call.

The script used by the phoners allowed clients to express their fears about possible computer errors. Answers to 30 possible questions were included in the script to reassure clients, ('counter-considerations'). The telephone is in fact the only medium that allows you to answer people's questions as they ask them. This is particularly important when selling complex banking services.

The successful test calls gave rise to a programme which sold products during the same call – not only the 'Billing System' but also a credit card issued by the bank (another monthly payable service) and an automatic savings account.

The computer provided accurate lists and identified which services to offer which individual. An additional service was offered to clients even if they had refused the 'Billing System'. All three services were offered to 70 per cent of people called, thus lowering the cost per service sold.

Applied to the whole range of clients, the programme continued to produce impressive results. The response rate was about 20 per cent and the cost per order was less than £5.21. The bank tried other selling techniques to increase the number of its client accounts. It found out, however, that telemarketing was particularly successful in these two areas.

First, the cost per new account opened was less than through any other medium tested. Second, an effective programme of cross-selling generated a large number of accounts that built up revenues and which would not have been opened otherwise. The few managers who thought that selling on the telephone was not a good idea for the bank's image were reassured not only by clients' responses, but also by the positive results of a study run by an independent organisation.

The people surveyed during the study gave very high marks to the telephoners for the information they provided and for their politeness. Furthermore, this survey revealed that more than half of the people surveyed who agreed to participate in the billing system would have refused this offer had they not received the bank President's pre-recorded message first.

The successes of British banks on the phone

Getting customers to the branches

A large British bank decided, in the context of developing a large regional office, to contact a target of selected prospects located within one specific zone of the bank. The objective was to promote the opening of chequeing and savings accounts. It took four weeks to develop a very precise script which was conceived and tested over several hundred calls, in order to consider all possible objections and develop all possible answers.

Their strategy was to identify proximity and satisfaction as being principal criteria of choice for a new bank. The list was selected by analysing the catchment zone and competitors in order to identify the most likely addresses. The objective was to generate a traffic of potential clients interested in opening an account and to capitalise on each visit.

The results were astounding. According to the marketing director of that bank: 'no other promotional medium than the telephone can produce such immediate results for the number of opened accounts in an agency'. Nearly 20 per cent of contacted people agreed to visit the bank, and 75 per cent of these opened an account.

Direct sales of a new product: product approach

The objective of a second telephone operation was to promote an automatic savings scheme which allowed people to accumulate savings without effort. This was done through transfers from their bank account to a high interest savings account. Telephoners, working from a pre-tested script, offered clients this automatic savings account. A mailing had already been sent to all clients in order to offer them the same product.

Clients appreciated the personal telephone contact and were very proud of being contacted by their bank. They had the perception that the bank was interested in them as individuals. The mailing generated 2.1 per cent response of clients who decided to use this automatic saving scheme. On the telephone, the response rate exceeded 20 per cent. Furthermore, in addition to the direct result, the telephone created increased traffic to the branches since an important number of clients visited the local agencies to discuss these products. About 12 per cent additional contracts were signed at the branch.

Overall, 35 per cent of clients contacted agreed to use this scheme. This is a significant example of a multi-media campaign where the telephone complements mailings, billboard advertising and point of sale material in the branches. The marketing specialist must also consider synergy of all media. There is no miracle medium capable of solving all your problems in marketing.

Direct sales of services tailored to client needs

When looking at client address lists, I believe that when one wants to sell complementary services, clients should be put into five groups:

- Group 1: clients with 'dormant' accounts
- Group 2: clients with an active account but no savings account
- Group 3: clients with an active savings account, but who don't use other bank services (credit card, etc.)
- Group 5: clients using most of the bank's services.

The phone's cross-selling objective will be to move clients from Group 1 to Group 2, those from Group 2 to Group 3, etc. This approach will optimise the sale of banking products while keeping in mind the needs of the client.

As a result a new job description will arise within banking groups: Direct Marketing Manager. This individual will work on a PC with an automatic dialler and telemarketing software including these functions:

- prospect management
- on the screen script
- diary
- reporting
- mail follow-up and printer.

A professional approach

These successes reflect a productive and creative telemarketing campaign. Future telemarketing users must keep four things in mind.

1   Best results come from campaigns structured with care. Telemarketing is not a part-time activity designed to prevent trainees from becoming lazy. It is a discipline. Professor Levitt, Marketing Professor at Harvard, describes the precision system: 'One can apply production line approaches to service activities, and these approaches bring as much productivity improvement as they did to the production line which improved the work of the coach manufacturer'.

   A successful campaign needs a set of production notes, rigorous controls, continuous supervision and training for phoners so that they pay as much attention to what they hear as to what they say. The script must present a message, anticipate questions, answer them, and capitalise on the situation within the shortest possible time. Only through this structured approach can campaigns result in lowered sales costs.

2   For most campaigns (and particularly when cross-selling), the telephone must be supported by other media. Multi-media campaigns present a real synergy, and the performance of each individual medium is increased.

   Within today's context, where banks try to demonstrate that they are geared towards customer care, synergy is created by the telephone so that this tool is a valuable one within a multi-media marketing mix.

3   Marketing managers must not think that they will alienate clients by calling them. Studies confirmed the results of a long series of tests designed to measure consumer attitudes: new clients welcome dialogue on the telephone. In that respect, the telephone is better geared towards consumers than other media.

4   The best uses of telemarketing are in multi-product approaches geared to client targets. This renews relations with the bank. Anything which creates more traffic at the branches will result in new accounts being opened.

Banking applications in telemarketing

● Selling products and services.
   – cross-selling banking services
   – blank accounts
   – credit cards

- cash cards
- automatic savings accounts
- savings accounts
- Selling credit cards.
- Generating prospects/applications for opening accounts.
- Generating prospects/applications for loans.
- Selling treasury bonds.
- Conducting market surveys to develop new products.
- Generating potential users of direct debit of salaries.
- Generating users for financial advisory services.
- The most successful uses are cross-selling of banking products to clients who do not use all the bank's services.
- Opening new accounts is best suited to the telephone.

6

THE TELEPHONE AND CONSUMER GOODS

Maintaining product awareness with retailers

Telephone contact is advantageous in this area for several reasons:

- to familiarise the retailers with you and your products
- to increase the frequency of contact between the manufacturer and the retailer
- to increase the likelihood of retailers stocking your products in preference to the competitors'.

It is clear that a wholesaler who is selling three competitive products has no particular reason to promote to retailers one product in preference to another. A wholesaler delivers what the retailer orders. Running telephone campaigns with the retailers makes it possible to promote your own product over the competitors'. However, even if the brand is known, this type of 'new product' selling has to be done in stages.

First call

- Presenting the product, its benefits.
- Agreeing a telephone appointment for another call.
- Sending a limited quantity of the product or a sample.

Second call

- Closing the sale.

The type of campaign which gives the best results in terms of quantity of orders obtained is to get the retailer to listen to a prerecorded message of about one and a half minutes explaining the themes of the forthcoming advertising campaign. Stress that it is important to order immediately so he/she will have some available stock.

It should be stressed that sales of unknown products and brands to unknown clients (prospects) are very difficult to achieve. The retailer who does not know you will be difficult to convince. Using the telephone will create a first element of trust. Also, using a cassette to describe the campaign inspires confidence in the retailers.

Some promotional incentive must be offered to facilitate these initial sales (eg. gifts, or price reduction above a certain quantity ordered). This kind of promotion facilitates direct sales on the telephone because it gives a reason for the call. Direct selling on the phone should be accompanied by some form of promotion which will answer the objection: 'Why have you called me on the phone, a letter could have served just as well or your sales person could have discussed this with me at the next visit?.'

Example

The objective was to make retailers aware of a new product brought out by an existing brand on behalf of wholesalers who are very involved with the campaign. An initial test was run involving 1,000 points of sale.

- *A mailshot including a sample of the product was sent; and*
- *Telephone calls offering to take orders on special promotional terms were made.*

Result

- *54 per cent of people placed orders.*
- *The sales company got to know the retail clients much better (the wholesaler is sometimes a screen between the manufacturer and the retailer).*
- *Retailers' stocks were established at a higher level, increasing market share in relationship to the competitors.*

Example

For a company in the ready-made clothes business, the objective was to get retailers to stock their products in preparation for the next advertising campaign. Getting retailers to listen to a cassette describing the advertising campaign which was to take place on the radio convinced the retailers of the need, which they had not understood previously, of having stocked up enough to satisfy clients influenced by the advertising campaign.

A month before the start of the campaign, and in a period of one week, 1,500 retailers were briefed about the format of the campaign and 58 per cent of them placed an order.

Result

- *58 per cent of retailers placed an order.*
- *Better lines of communication were established between the brand name and the retailers who felt they were especially privileged in being informed of new releases.*
- *Maximum activation of the whole sales network.*

Communicating sales support information and re-ordering

The telephone can also be used to get to know how the sales of your products are developing, and to take advantage of the survey to obtain repeat orders.

Surveys have shown that a sales person selling consumer products when visiting clients will spend the time in these ways:

- 30 per cent on the way
- 17 per cent waiting
- 10 per cent off-work
- 8 per cent on administration
- 18 per cent controlling stocks at client sites
- only 17 per cent making sales at client premises.

These figures should be enough to promote the use of the telephone, especially when a company has the feeling that their sales people are just registering orders rather than acting as real commercial prospectors, or if they do not have time to visit the retailer prospects.

In an organisation where sales are made through sales people selling your own brand only, and are paid with a fixed salary and commission, I recommend setting up pairs operating 'visit–telephone', ie. sales person/phoner. The sales person's task will be to deal with important clients and to locate new ones. The phoner will deal with small clients geographically dispersed offering low potential.

Telephone contact with the clients must take place between

visits from the sales team. It is therefore necessary to plan combined sales person–phoner campaigns. Various criteria have to be considered:

- the number of sales per client
- the geographical position of the client
- the potential level of sales which can be achieved.

Prospective clients should be graded 1 to 5, from not very important (or 'cool') to very important (or 'hot'). In this way, sales people visit every month large clients with a grade of 5, and once a year the small clients with a grade of 1. The phoners never call clients with a grade 5, but every month call the clients with a grade 1, every two months those with a grade 2, every three months clients graded 3, and every six months clients graded 4.

The following system can also be considered. According to the level of sales obtained, the client will receive a grade from 1 (low) to 5. The same type of grading will be applied according to the prospect's location. The prospect's potential for placing orders will equally be given a grade.

The number of points are added together. You can then decide to visit clients between 12 and 15 points. Between 9 and 12 points, a mix of telephone calls between visits can be set up. Between 6 and 9 points, two to three calls will be made between visits. Between 3 and 6 points, the client will be visited once a year and contact by phone will be the priority.

These figures and suggestions are given as examples only, as the rate at which telephone visits are made depends to a great extent on the quality of the visiting sales force in the company. Bear in mind that telephone sales, even for repeat orders, are sometimes resented by the sales team as sales people feel they are in competition with their own company.

- They may resent the fact that a telephone sales team who does not have ten years' experience of the product manages to take as many repeat sales as they do.
- If small clients are processed on the phone, the sales person will have to prospect for new clients, will have to cover a larger area, and will have to handle other products, all of which generates resistance to change.
- The sales person will have to visit large clients more often, and this will oblige him/her to negotiate, to contact a new set of people, to actually sell and not simply pick up orders. . . Again a change of habits!

The company and the good sales people will benefit, however, as their sales figures go up. The system works best for all companies whose sales follow the 80/20 rule. Twenty per cent of turnover will come from handling 80 per cent of clients mainly on the phone. Eighty per cent of turnover will come from 20 per cent of the clients who are visited.

Example

A company in the cosmetics industry wished to test the principle of telephone selling of products used by consumers, retailed by small client hairdressers. Contact was made in two stages. The first call involved mentioning the usual contact with the sales person and asking for an evaluation of available stocks, and making arrangements for a second call within 48 hours.

On the second call, the sales person tried to close the order. In this example, 75 per cent of hairdressers contacted placed an order; this was very slightly less than the usual monthly order obtained by sales people (77 per cent).

Example

There are extreme cases such as Primel S.A., the most important French dealer in seafood, who make 2,500 phone calls a day using 50 phoners. Their target is 12,000 clients, of which 6,000 are active (restaurants, fishmongers, wholesalers, and wholesalers of deep-frozen fish). Two sales people work in conjunction with the 50 phoners and visit the most important clients.

The results are spectacular: 1,300 orders each day (50 per cent conversion rate) and an annual turnover of £41.66 million. Trust is the basis of this kind of sale, as no written confirmation is made.

It is my belief that most companies selling consumer goods will set up teams of sales people/phoners constituting real telephone sales commandos. The sales person will then become more of a specialised consultant.

Having this kind of telesales team in a company provides answers to other commercial problems, eg. tests for new products, and fast information return from the market. It can prove particularly useful in the following sample situations.

Example

1   *One of the best sales people in the company happens to be absent for a prolonged period. What is to be done? Divide his/her territory*

between the other sales people? Hire a new sales person? Visit the large clients only? The telephone is an answer. The telesales team can keep that territory alive, while the other sales people negotiate with the large clients, a telephone campaign can be organised to contact all the small clients.

2 *A competitor has launched a new product on the market and you have to respond very quickly. To operate through the wholesaler will take time, especially as the competitor's advertising campaign may be taking place. The telephone will be a fast and efficient answer to promote a new product directly to the retailers without interfering with your visiting sales team.*

3 *Your newspaper, radio or TV campaign has been more successful than you could have hoped for. Everybody wants the product you have launched and the most enterprising clients call you directly. You know that for one who does call, there are ten who do not. The telephone will, in the minimum possible time, allow you to contact your clients and have them re-order your stock.*

4 *The country experiences a sudden heatwave and demand for your type of product increases dramatically. The telephone will allow you to accelerate deliveries to cafés, hotels, restaurants, shops, etc. where they are most required.*

It is important that the company who wishes to set up telephone contacts with clients, even small ones, should realise that some opposition may arise from their own sales people and sometimes from the head of sales, who may feel that some of their power is being withdrawn. The success of any project depends on the involvement and assistance of the sales team. Experience shows that every time a telesales operation is installed, the sales team, eventually, are totally satisfied. It is therefore important to involve the sales team in the decision to set up a telephone system. The sales team must understand that the telephone is a support to their activity, exactly like mailshots.

7

THE TELEPHONE AND THE PUBLISHING INDUSTRY

Direct sales of subscriptions

A case study

In 1968, Norman Cousins, a well-known writer and publisher, wanted to launch a new weekly magazine which was to be called 'Saturday Review'. He met Murray Roman who convinced him to take a considerable risk: to launch 'Saturday Review' by phone using the name of Norman Cousins alone, before the first issue of the magazine had even been designed. The magazine was only an idea. Murray Roman adapted the telemessage system. Norman Cousins' voice was recorded with a message that had been worked out in great detail to achieve maximal impact.

The system was excellent: a phoner would start the conversation: 'Good morning, Mr Davis, my name is Nancy Young, and I am calling on behalf of Norman Cousins. I have a message especially pre-recorded for you from Norman Cousins. This message is going to last two minutes. Can I put it on now, Mr Davis? Do you have the time?'

If the prospect answered 'yes' or 'who is Norman Cousins?', the message was put on; if he/she answered 'no' or 'who is that?', the message was not played. Tests showed that people who did not know at all who Norman Cousins was would only have a very low potential for subscribing to 'Saturday Review', and it was important not to waste time on them.

After the message, the phoner would close the offer. The list of prospects had been selected by taking into account the lifestyle of the prospects. Lists had been bought from specialist brokers of people with a high income, cultural interests, and a high level of education. As a result of this method, 40 per cent of prospects agreed to subscribe and three quarters of these subscribed for three years. Cousins' telemessage programme is now running at a rate of more than six million calls with the same degree of success.

In France in 1988, the cost per subscriber obtained through mailings was rising steeply. The publisher of a daily newspaper is prepared to invest 50 per cent of the price of the subscription into gaining new subscribers, which means that, for instance, on a yearly subscription of £156.25, £78.13 will be spent trying to increase the number of subscribers. So the objective for telesales is to create a new subscriber for less than £78.13. If the same calculation is made for weekly and monthly newspapers, a limit of costs for the creation of a subscriber will be £52.08 for a weekly, and £26.04 for a monthly publication. Taking as a worst case scenario the telemarketing cost for each lead as £1, it is therefore necessary to generate:

- one subscriber for every 75 leads in the case of a daily newspaper (1.3 per cent success rate)
- one subscriber for every 50 leads in the case of a weekly newspaper (2 per cent success rate)
- one subscriber for every 25 leads in the case of a monthly publication.

This shows clearly that it is more difficult to get cost-effective results for a monthly publication than it is for a daily. The work done on selecting lists will be the key factor in making the campaign cost-effective. It is not possible to work from a telephone directory or badly targeted lists. For a daily newspaper, analyse locations where home delivery is easy, as this is an important selling feature. For weekly or monthly publications, promoting competitions may attract new subscribers, and exchanging lists with other publishers will mean you have a well-targeted list to work from.

Renewing subscriptions

A sizeable proportion of subscribers to a publication does not renew its subscription after having been sent a mailshot. It is a shame to give up these previous subscribers, even if the mailshot has not given results. The telephone is then the only means of communication which, because it generates a dialogue, can successfully generate a renewal of the subscription.

The result of subscription renewal campaigns on the phone can be between 10 and 40 per cent of the total number of people contacted. I believe that telemessage systems will eventually increase such results. In the case of *L'Expansion*, a French economics magazine, a subscription renewal campaign carried out with a telemessage from Jean Boissonnat, a very well-known French journalist, gave a result 30 per cent better than with a professional phoner negotiating on the phone without the help of the telemessage. However, a telemessage recorded by an unknown person does not give such good results.

Another element contributing to the success of telephoning subscribers is the subscription renewal cycle chosen by the publisher. For instance, if the call comes after six mailshot prompts to renew subscriptions, the overall result of the successive mailing-telephone campaign is not as good as a cycle of three mailings followed by a telephone call, then followed by two mailings.

The best time to use the telephone in the cycle of actions is when the subscription stops. As soon as the subscriber stops receiving the publication, the telephone will obtain the maximum results. The three elements determining the result of a subscription renewal campaign are:

- the frequency of calls
- the technique chosen (telemessage or none)
- the cycle of mailshots/phone calls.

In the case of *L'Expansion*, the telephone campaign resulted in an 8 to 12 per cent success rate when targeting the list of previous subscribers. In the case of *Le Point* (a general information magazine), the score was 18 per cent after six mailings, which had already generated 63 per cent renewals.

It is obvious that telephone campaigns for subscription renewals can be cost-effective for monthly as well as weekly or daily publications. It is true that a telephone campaign will be more cost-effective for a daily than a weekly and especially than a monthly publication. However, the renewal of a subscription obtained by phone for a monthly with a low subscription price will still be lower than the recruitment of a new subscriber through any other known method.

Selling book collections

Companies like Time Life have successfully developed a telephone sales system giving the best results on non-qualified targets, as the campaign is made on cold calling telephone directory lists.

The success of the system relies on the frequency of calls and the concept of book collections. On 100 calls made, eight people agreed to receive a book at the price of £12.50, for instance, and to have the option to send it back within two weeks and get a refund if they do not like the book. In fact, on average three people will keep the book and pay for it.

The cost of the campaign is £104.16 for ten hours work, and the sales generated are 3 × £12.50 = £37.50.

At this point the publisher is making a loss, but next month the second book will be offered to the three clients on the same terms and 2.6 people will order. The cost of the campaign is £4.16 and the number of sales generated is 2.6 × £12.50 = £32.50.

Over twelve to eighteen months, knowing that the clients' interest has been aroused, Time Life will invest about £150 to generate a total sales of over £400. In addition to this, the prospect list has now been enriched by *qualified prospects*. Time Life is in a position to run such campaigns because the company can invest very large amounts before getting their pay-back over the year. Other companies use this system to generate successful sales of book collections to clients who had stopped buying their products.

On average, 20 to 30 per cent of people contacted buy the collection, which means the cost of sale is less than £10. This rate is consistently found in the mail-order business for companies selling textiles or house furniture. There again, the rhythm of the work done on the phone is a condition of cost-effectiveness and therefore of the success of the campaigns.

If phoners targeting consumers work at the rate of less than ten conversations per hour, there will be cost problems. That is why the setting up of an in-house integrated system must be organised very carefully. If your in-house team works at the rate of five to six useful contacts per hour on targeted consumers, it will be in your interest to ask a telemarketing services company to run your campaign. You can also consult professional consultants to improve your own in-house operation and increase the results and cost-effectiveness of your campaigns. Without professional advice or know-how, it is very easy to lose considerable sums of money in this area of telesales.

Conditions for success in the publishing industry

The difficulties that any publisher will come across are the following:

- How to set up a phoning script with a creative approach which will not just be a repeat of your last mailshot.
- How to manage the turnover of phoners.
- How to obtain the help of a highly specialised supervisor.
- How to stimulate the telesales team without going into high-pressure selling.
- How to manage the irregularities in the frequency of calls.

The keys to success are found in the way those problems are addressed, which should start with consulting experienced professionals.

I consider that the setting up of an in-house telemarketing team in the publishing industry meets with a major problem concerning the hours at which calls have to be made to contact targeted prospects in their home. Phoners have to work between 5 pm and 8.30 pm and on Saturdays, which is often difficult to manage within the company. That is why subcontracting is often the best solution.

The example of publications, like *L'Express*, which have an in-house team is interesting. *L'Express* increasingly applies to an external services subcontractor to increase the frequency of calls at a cost which actually turns out to be less than that of their in-house operation.

8

THE TELEPHONE AND DIRECT MAIL SELLING

Obtaining and processing calls

Increase your clients by 25 per cent

The large French mail-order businesses have understood that a well-displayed telephone number in their catalogue or through their mailings can increase the number of orders received directly by mail. Publicising the telephone number increases the normal average response to mailings by 25 per cent.

People are increasingly sensitive to oral communication – you only have to consider how many written communications and telephone calls you have personally had or made in the last two months. It is highly probable that you phone more than you write. This fact is also true for your potential clients.

Increase the volume of sales by 50 per cent

In-coming telephone calls will generate 25 per cent more orders than mailings alone, but there is an extra benefit in the possibility of increased or crossed sales.

When answering in-coming calls, a phoner who has been carefully and methodically trained will have the opportunity to offer additional products to those being ordered by the client – a tie to go with a shirt or the new range of beauty products to go with the perfume. This way you can increase the level of sales for each order.

If 100 clients send a written order, you can consider that the telephone will make it possible for you to take 25 extra orders, ie. a total of 125 orders. But the volume of orders received on the phone should be at least 25 per cent higher with the opportunity for extra selling, which means that out of these 125 clients you will have the possibility of increasing the overall amount of sales to 150 per cent of the original sales.

The importance of organisation

The organisation of the phone team receiving in-coming calls is vital. Too few good phoners to receive calls and a casual set up will not be successful.

An important aspect of organising a telephone system is to work out the number of phoners that should be used. It is difficult to get the right balance between the number of phoners on an in-coming call team, and the number of calls actually coming in. It is vital that potential clients should be able to make contact without difficulty and without any undue waiting, and important to have enough operators receiving calls, but, on the other hand, if the volume of calls is less than expected the cost of idle personnel will come high.

That is why it is very important to have a good assessment of the number of calls that will be generated by your promotional efforts to make your phone number known. However good your estimates, there will always be seasonal variations, and even in the course of one day the volume of calls will not be regular. It is important if your phoners' team is to be cost-effective to have the rate of calling above a certain limit. That is why I recommend the combination of in-coming and out-going calling as described below.

Going ahead with out-going phoning

The 'allocated time' approach

Many mail-order businesses hesitate before they undertake out-going calling on their client list, even though this method gives very good results, with a level of unit sale higher than for normal orders. It is important to know that with out-going calling it is possible to produce 30 to 40 per cent orders on a client list. The 'allocated time' approach is a method which combines in-coming and out-going calling within the same organisation system.

The objective is to organise a telephone operation using a fixed number of phoners who will, as they follow a pre-defined diary, operate on out-going calling or answer in-coming calls, but will not be doing these two things within the same hour. Effective supervision is vital to the success of such a system. Even if it is possible to allocate phoners to out-going and in-coming phoning according to the volume of calls estimated, supervisors must be in a position to optimise the activity of the whole team.

For instance, there will be times when in a team of ten phoners everyone will be answering in-coming calls, and there will be other times during which three phoners will be answering calls and seven will be making out-going calls. If it were to happen that the volume of in-coming calls was higher than expected, three of the seven phoners making out-going calls could immediately start taking calls instead. It is the system of allocated times which makes it possible to optimise the performance of phoners while ensuring that your clients are not kept waiting. Also, you will not be taking the risk, as you would with five or six phoners taking in-coming calls only, of having inactive times or clients being dissatisfied because your number is always busy.

Conditions for success

For out-going phoning to be successful, it is necessary to follow a strategy which is not based on trying to get an order on the phone at that moment, but that will create a client database that responds to ordering on the phone.

In the long run, your company will have a database of a few hundred thousand clients who wish to be called regularly to be kept informed of special promotional events. In addition to this, it is possible to optimise the cost-effectiveness of out-going calling by selecting specific products on which promotional offers can be made with acceptable margins. Also, the hourly rate of calling for the phoners must generate enough orders per hour of work to make this approach cost-effective. A well-trained and organised phoner must obtain ten to twelve useful contacts per hour of calling with a 30 per cent conversion rate and a level for each sale that is higher than the average order received by mail.

The cost of a telephone contact will not be more than a pound on average for an in-house telemarketing operation integrated in a mail-order business. So the cost per order should not be more than £3 to £4 on out-going calling, which is not excessive if you consider these are all extra orders. What is more, in a system organised around allocated times the costs per sale will be even lower.

Case study

For a large mail-order business having a telephone system organised to receive calls from the whole of France, experience has shown that telemarketing on out-going calling was not only accepted by the clients, but welcomed by them and highly cost-effective.

The objective was to contact by phone clients who had, through a previous contact (made in writing or on the phone), expressed their willingness to be called on the phone to be informed of special promotions. The strategy adopted for calling was more to inform clients than to attempt to sell systematically.

This soft selling formula generated 40 per cent orders with an average unit price of £73, producing more than £200 sales per hour of phoners' work.

As it had been found that the in-coming call answering system would, because of the low level of activity during January, February, May, June and July, be working at 70 per cent capacity only, it was possible, by getting phoners to make out-going calls during these slow months, to obtain, per year and per phoner, 500 hours of out-going calling generating £36,458.33 from each phoner.

Using the telephone to sell credit cards for a large European mail-order business

Experience has shown that a client of a mail-order business holding a credit card of the mail-order company orders on average three times more than they had ordered during the year prior to obtaining the card. Therefore, it is extremely profitable to advertise your credit card and to promote its use by your clients to generate extra revenue.

Among the means at your disposal to recruit cardholders among your clients (such as catalogues, mailshots, etc.), the telephone is a choice weapon both in in-coming and out-going calling.

What often holds the client back is the automatic withdrawal of money from his or her account, and then having to send the authorising signature by return. The telephone is a good way of overcoming this consideration. On inbound calling, the rate of success will vary between 15 and 30 per cent from one organisation to another.

Phoners answering in-coming calls will sometimes find it difficult when a client is calling to place an order to sell him a credit card in addition to his order. As you know, having two different objectives in the same message is always difficult.

On out-going calling, the rate of success will vary between 20 and 25 per cent of clients contacted, which according to the chosen method will mean a cost of £12 to £25.

If the mail-order business is organised with local offices in each area and using in-house personnel, the cost of recruiting credit cardholders is about £12. Using the services of a third party company the cost reaches £24, which is the average cost of such a recruitment when all the mix of media are put together. So it is clear that an in-house team is the best way.

Setting up an efficient system that will generate such positive results requires professional methods:

- constant supervision
- a structured telephone script
- in-depth training of the phoners
- quality control.

9

THE TELEPHONE AND PHARMACEUTICAL LABORATORIES

Changes in the medical sector

The increasing costs of communication have meant laboratories need to use new ways of communicating with doctors.

The number of doctors has doubled in the last ten years. The number of pharmaceutical representatives has stayed the same. To follow the trend it would have been necessary for the number of pharmaceutical representatives to be increased by 10 per cent per year, which for each network would mean increased costs of between £120,000 and £200,000. In addition to this, personnel turnover within a pharmaceutical representative's network means that at any given time 10 to 20 per cent of areas are vacant.

To counter this, and the inflation in the cost of pharmaceutical representative's visits, laboratories must, within the context of increased competition, find new means of communication: telephone, video, teleconferences, videotex, electronic mail. Distance communication must act as a support to visits by the pharmaceutical reps without creating any interference. These methods should not follow the rules of pharmaceutical representatives' visits: new creative approaches need to be devised.

The search for more efficient communication leads to recommendations being made to the following groups:

- doctors
- prescription chemists
- dental surgeons
- wholesalers.

These groups can in turn be split down to:

- general practitioners
- specialists
- young doctors
- group practices
- hospital doctors
- non-visited
- refusing to be visited
- residing abroad
- etc.

The telephone must be used in the following areas:

- medical information
- information feedback
- pharmacology vigilance
- invitation to an event
- statistical results of clinical studies
- surveys – studies – polls
- . . . following our orders/questions arising out of communication actions (media, etc. . . .).

With chemists, the telephone must be used in the following areas:

- surveys
- presenting new products
- information concerning packaging, dosages, etc. . . .

A systematic, creative approach

The strategy for communicating on the telephone in the medical field relies on a systematically creative approach. Only extreme care in preparing actions will lead to success. Operations should run through three stages. Organising the operation in this way will ensure each action is cost-effective.

- Make test calls and adjust the programme.
- Extend the number of calls and control cost-effectiveness (market testing).
- Extend the programme to the selected target (nationwide or locally).

The design of the programme must include the following stages:

- studying the product
- training supervisors
- creating the script
- pre-testing the script on 300 prospects
- setting up control procedures
- organising follow-up and coordination.

This first series of actions will make it possible to measure two basic elements for the next stage in the programme:

- the quality of the message
- acceptance from the target.

Creating the programme requires four to six weeks of work. Fifty complete telephone presentations must have been made to prove that the message is accepted by the target. At the end of that period, in consultation with the laboratory, you need to:

- finalise a script accompanied by a recorded conversation
- obtain a measure of the message's rate of acceptance by the target.

The laboratory can then decide whether to carry on with the second phase.

To carry out the market testing, the laboratory must choose a test area big enough to make significant statistical measurements of the cost-effectiveness of a telephone campaign.

This market testing should reach 300 doctors and be made under the control of the Production Manager assisted by three people:

- a supervisor for quantitative control
- a person monitoring conversations and recordings
- a person in charge of managing call sheets.

Phoners can be selected among three categories as follows, according to the specifics of the programme:

- professional phoners
- pharmaceutical representatives
- medical doctors.

After this first operation covering the test area, it is possible to determine, by measuring sales results, the cost-effectiveness of telemarketing action. Only with a complete understanding of all the financial and marketing figures can it be recommended to extend nationally.

This whole approach may seem cumbersome and slow but short cuts should not be made if cost-effective results are to be achieved.

Which methodology to use?

Work should take place in stages, following a blueprint as follows:

Meeting concerning the market/the product/the strategy: the telemarketing team must meet with the lab management representatives to get to know the product and its market. During that meeting the approach strategy must be selected.

Writing the script: the creative team must write the telephone-call script to cover the whole development of a telephone contact.

Designing models of control sheets: the telemarketing team must design special control sheets showing the result of each telephone call and giving a cumulative picture of data collected as well as a report on phoners' performances.

Selecting the lists: the laboratory must supply the telemarketing team with prospects' details on sticky labels to carry out the first telephone surveys.

Training of supervisors: the telemarketing account manager must train the team of telemarketing supervisors in the product and the script before preliminary tests are carried out.

Preliminary test: the team carrying out preliminary tests will make a series of calls to measure the quality of the script and take note of all considerations expressed by the targets. Calls will be recorded and replayed by the creative team who will then modify the script as necessary until the best possible scenario is obtained. This period of testing and modification will supply all the necessary information to set up the campaign under the best conditions.

Script meeting: a second meeting will have to take place with the management of the laboratory to assess the script and the corresponding recording. If the laboratory asks for major modifications in the script, pre-testing must again be done until everything is settled perfectly.

Phoners' training: the phoners' team will have to be trained carefully with both simulated and real calls under the control of supervisors. The people who need training include:

- production manager
- assistant to the manager
- supervisor (quantitative control of results)
- controller (qualitative control and listening in)
- person in charge of lists.

Case studies

One of the first cases in which the telephone was used in the pharmaceutical industry was in France. An improvised company, started up by previous members of the management of Medec, had as its objective to promote a new vaccine with a target of 50,000 MDs. The phoners had been recruited from third and fourth year medical students, and presented themselves as doctors, which was an indefensible lie. The medical profession reacted vigorously against this approach.

At that time, however, in the United States, laboratories such as SKF, MSD and Johnson regularly used the telephone to communicate with doctors. However, to develop the use of the telephone in France meant adapting it to the French mentality and not simply copying American methods.

The first real success story in promoting pharmaceuticals on the phone occurred in 1981 by the Human Pharm laboratories. They used a telemessage to launch a pregnancy test product targeted at chemists. The phoner started the conversation and suggested that the prospect listened to a 30 second message specially recorded by the doctor in charge concerning this new test product. The telemessage provided three benefits:

- no corruption of the information and guaranteed precision
- a concise description
- a powerful impact through the authority of the speaker as a medical expert.

This approach was run over a fifteen-day period contacting 10,000 chemists, 98 per cent of whom agreed to listen to the message. It achieved the remarkable result that fifteen days after the media launch of the product, there was *an absolute guarantee* that the 10,000 leading chemists in France knew of the product and of all its characteristics. This could not have been achieved by any other method.

The cost of this campaign was fifteen times cheaper than the eventual cost of visits made by a team of pharmaceutical reps covering the same population, which furthermore would have been impossible to achieve in a fifteen-day period.

10

THE TELEPHONE
AND FINANCIAL
SERVICES COMPANIES

Financial services: a plus for selling

Offering financial facilities has become a means of developing a market, and appears to be a determining element in making sales. When a piece of equipment is targeted to a given group, and is offered with specifically adapted financial facilities, that piece of equipment becomes more accessible to the market. Applying this simple fact has made fortunes for financial services companies. The development of these companies took place as a result of the constraints imposed by the large banking networks who, either because of regulations or their own inertia, were not in a position to offer the same terms as companies who specialised in financing equipment goods for private users. Most of these financial services companies are owned by industrial groups.

The big banking networks have started to be much more aware and active in providing their users with ways of buying a car or household equipment, but companies which finance the buying of cars and which have close ties with the manufacturer have also become increasingly active.

Example

The success achieved by ECS (European Computer Systems) shows the importance of financing facilities in the development of sales. ECS was started about fifteen years ago by J L Bouchard who had previously been part of the IBM management team and who understood earlier than anyone else the importance of offering credit facilities in the sale of computer hardware. ECS specialised in financing IBM computers to meet the needs of user companies and to offer solutions which IBM did not provide. It does so more dynamically than companies which have traditionally specialised in financing industrial equipment.

With the help of a highly motivated sales team, ECS expanded to a level of sales of £500 million.

In the area of industrial goods, selling with the help of financial services is also an efficient tool for expansion. In these approaches telemarketing plays a key part in acquiring both client loyalty and new clients. Selling financial services needs a completely different approach from other types of selling methods, insofar as more and more organisations have become aware of the importance of possessing their own financial services system.

The credit card approach

In the last few years credit card systems have been spectacularly developed. The large retail companies created their own credit cards with a view to acquiring client loyalty and to save the third-party commissions paid on the original credit cards. All large department stores will have between 200,000 and 1.5 million cardholders, representing several million consumers.

Example

Peugeot decided to issue their own credit card from their own financial company, Credipar. This was a first in the vehicle manufacturing industry as Credipar also distributes a bank card so now there is a new bank card in the Peugeot name. (Credipar was created for Peugeot clients.) This means that Peugeot clients, unlike Fiat or Ford clients, acquire with the Credipar card a proper bank card, which will consolidate client loyalty for Peugeot. For Credipar it is an opportunity to sell more credit facilities as this card is offered to any buyer of a Peugeot car, whether or not the acquisition was financed by Credipar.

Half the people who buy cars need credit facilities and half the people buying Peugeot cars using credit facilities will obtain these facilities from Credipar. This means Credipar has a 25 per cent market share of Peugeot car buyers.

It would seem that in the future we will either be seeing a number of credit cards which will be independent of the bank card, or we will see bank cards that will be tied in with brand names in the same way as Peugeot and Credipar.

In the first of these cases the number of points at which the card can be used becomes limited. In the second case the cost of the card to the consumer could be higher. That is the case of the Peugeot Credipar bank card; money can be drawn at bank cash dispensers at extra cost to the user. However, the Peugeot owner can also use this card to make purchases in any establishment that accepts bank cards.

In the context of this increasingly aggressive competition, financial services companies must make increasing efforts at marketing. Telemarketing has shown that worthwhile results can be obtained when selling financial services.

Selling to potential clients

There is a huge potential for creating new cardholders in big organisations as these companies often have millions of clients who do not use the card promoted by the distribution company.

To increase the number of cardholders, financial companies must promote the benefits of their card to their clients, who constitute a target of 'prospects' for the card. This can be done in three ways:

- selling the card in the shop premises
- selling the card through mailings
- selling the card on the phone.

When a sales point exists, as in the case of a department store, card employees can be motivated to sell the card. Some large retailers have managed to sell tens of thousands of cards by allocating commissions to their employees on each card sold.

The second method for selling credit cards is mailshots directed at clients who have paid by cheque and whose addresses have been collected. This method is used by most card-issuing organisations with a 2 to 10 per cent cost-effectiveness, depending on the quality of the offer, the list and the professionalism with which the message has been put together.

A third method is to use telemarketing either on in-coming or out-going calling. For example, it can be used in following up a mailshot in which a telephone number has been promoted suggesting the prospect call in for more information. According to the quality of the approach, 40 to 50 per cent of clients approached will call in and a 20 per cent take-up rate can be obtained from the people who call.

The telephone is a means of selling on in-coming calls. Through out-going calling the telephone can be used as a call-back campaign following mailshots which is most cost-effective than mailshots alone.

The combination of mailshot plus telephone can give a score of 20 to 25 per cent. For most organisations offering credit cards the acceptable cost per new user will vary between £8 and £13. The cost of a mailing is of the order of 52p per prospect, which combined with telephone callbacks at £2.60 will achieve a 25 per cent conversion rate giving a cost of £12.50 per new cardholder.

The key to successful combined campaigns, mailshot plus phoning, depends on the quality of the presentation and the productivity of calls.

Selling to existing clients

Another way of providing volume of sales for credit card promoters is in the volume of sales made to each holder. Telemarketing is a valuable help here, as its interactive feature makes it possible to promote an assortment of products. Selling is then done not on a product approach but on a market approach, as an assortment of services corresponding to clients' needs are offered.

The telephone script will include a few questions at the beginning of the call so that the phoner can promote the product best suited to the client's profile. If that product is not accepted it will then be possible to shift towards another product or service.

This method makes it possible to increase a client's use of financial services. For instance, if a person is considering buying this or that piece of equipment the telephone will enable you to offer the most suitable credit terms. In addition to this, when clients are approaching the end of their payments under a financial scheme, telemarketing is the most suitable and cheapest way to make a new offer based on the client's new needs. Two combined approaches are then used as follows.

1 In the first stage the financial services company sends a

mailshot in the form of a card asking the client to phone their offices. The processing of in-coming calls is an opportunity to offer that client an opportunity to take up a fresh loan to meet any further needs she might have, offering her very special terms because of her proven reliability in repaying the first loan. If the client has no immediate needs, an overdraft facility can be offered to be used at any time she likes.

On average, 25 to 30 per cent of clients contacted will take up a fresh loan after they have repaid their initial loan. However, half of these will only accept the *offer* of an overdraft facility, which does not mean that they will take it up.

2 In a second stage, telemarketing can be used to contact 'sleeping prospects'.

The combined use of mailshot plus phoning on in-coming calls is thought to be the best method of soliciting clients who currently have outstanding loans. Out-going phoning can be used to contact people who have not called in after a mailshot (40 per cent), the objective then being to prompt them to call back later, rather than trying to sell anything on this call.

A case study

In the United States in 1977, the Montgomery Ward company had about twenty million credit cardholders through its 'Signature' subsidiary. Montgomery Ward owns a chain of large department stores; 'Signature' had decided to launch an 'Automobile Club' with multiple support, financing, and information services based on a $20 subscription for each member.

They decided to use telemarketing to convert the greatest possible number of credit cardholders into club members. However, the first tests showed that the telemarketing approach was not cost-effective on the complete client list of twenty million holders. A means had to be found to select the two or three million most favourable prospects from the list.

'Signature' considered that the minimum level for cost-effectiveness was the acquisition of 2.5 members per hour of calling and therefore $50 income for $20 cost. It was decided that 500 orders would be generated on the phone, and that this list of buyers would be scored and compared with the cardholders list, so the most favourable target segment could be selected. (Scoring is a method of analytical prospecting which makes it possible to extract the most favourable target segment from a large database of prospects containing various psychographic criteria.)

'Signature' had 80 available criteria for analysis in their database. The list of buyers (after 500 orders had been obtained) was compared with the overall database using those criteria to extract the three million cardholders most likely to be interested in the club product. During the tests made using this new list, phoning generated 2.7 sales per hour, an increase of practically 40 per cent on the original results. Phoning then became cost-effective. Over two years, three million homes were processed with a team of 100 phoners achieving 10,000 contacts per year per phoner. This resulted in 550,000 members being recruited on the phone for the automobile club over those two years. This operation was probably one of the most important sales campaigns achieved in the United States and the most instructive concerning telemarketing methods.

11

THE TELEPHONE AND INSTITUTIONS

Fund raising

Strategy

All non-profit organisations, whether they be sports clubs, trade unions or political parties, live off the subscriptions of their members and off the financial help obtained from organisations or private individuals. Prospecting for financial support, or fund raising, is a vital activity for most such organisations. The objectives of telemarketing when used for this type of campaign is to produce a multiplying effect on the impact of mailshots in combined operations. The telephone when used professionally will multiply the results obtained from a mailshot by a factor of three to ten. The list of targets used on the phone determines the level of success obtained in fund raising.

Telephone marketing is particularly effective on calling back people who have already contributed or on calling back previous subscribers to, for example, a sporting club. For instance in the case of a French football club, which had 6,000 subscribers, mailshots generated re-subscriptions of 5,000 subscribers. By following up the mailshot with phoning actions, 400 extra renewals were obtained from the 2,000 who had not responded; a 20 per cent conversion rate on the residual list.

The message is the second most important item in a successful strategy. In most cases, in the case of associations and clubs, the telemessage method is recommended, if a well-known personality is used as this gives an enhanced impact to the phone call.

The technical telemessage, which can on out-going phoning communicate a specific message recorded by a known personality to a population which can reach thousands of people, is a significant support when prospecting for fund raising. The phoner will start the conversation and suggest to the prospect that they should listen to a message especially addressed and recorded for them by this well-known personality. After the pre-recorded message has been played, the phoner continues the call to close. The pre-recorded message clearly must be perfect.

In addition to the impact of the personality used, the telemessage technique guarantees the quality of the wording and the intonation as careful testing is carried out in the recording studio. The credibility of the message is guaranteed by using a personality whose voice is well-known, so there can be no mistaking the truth of its origin. It is very important to select a personality who relates to the targeted population.

Sponsors for sports clubs

In 1984, I was consulted for a project aimed at launching a system in France by which companies could reserve boxes in a major football stadium. Company decision-makers would have the possibility of attending events in privileged VIP conditions. Most first division football clubs now offer such a prestigious service for companies who can reserve a box in the club's football stadium for their business contacts.

To launch this idea it was necessary to find within the 1,000 leading French companies 80 who would subscribe for an annual subscription of between £4,166 to £9,375 per year.

The telemarketing assignment was to organise a telemarketing campaign reaching the 1,000 leading companies in the Paris area. A pre-recorded message from the President of the football club was devised, which described the benefits obtained from the football club: 'Each subscriber will have a four-seat box reserved with access to the cocktail reception lounges and dining rooms where receptions take place with well-known personalities and managers of the club after the sporting event.' At the end of the message, which lasted 50 seconds, the phoner offered an option and invited each prospect to come and test the VIP service during the next match.

Out of 1,000 decision-makers contacted on the phone, 162 agreed to take the option and come for this sampling. The 80 boxes were sold the following month. Against an investment of less than £10,416 made in 1984, the club collected more than £500,000. In 1986 the VIP club sales rose to over £1.64 million, an amount which capped all the contributions from the other club sponsors and was the main source of private funding for the football club.

Similar campaigns were run by other French football clubs, with great success. In each of these, success was assured by three principles:

- A pre-recorded message from a well-known personality which gave credibility to the telephone approach.
- The commitment of the phoning teams with callbacks, follow-up, etc.
- Careful segmentation of the list to target according to the type of companies.

Campaigning for a political candidate

The American system

The first major telemarketing operation in support of a political campaign was the one undertaken by Murray Roman for J.F. Kennedy. This operation to promote favourable votes required the help of 20,000 helpers who called ten million American homes to engage in a dialogue to enhance the image of the candidate. People appreciate being communicated to directly by the candidate. When a handshake is not possible, a phone call is better than a leaflet or a mailshot. As it was impossible to convert ordinary helpers into telephone specialists, Murray Roman invented the pre-recorded telemessage. The part played by each helper was reduced to starting the call, pressing the button of the tape recorder, and, after playing the message, closing the call.

Two hundred supervisors from the committee for the election of J.F. Kennedy were trained by Murray Roman. These 200 supervisors in groups of ten took part in an intensive ten-day training in telephone skills. Each left the training with 100 tape recorders, 100 scripts and 100 copies of the recorded message. Each supervisor had to recruit 100 helpers which she would then train, in groups of ten, over two days. Each trained helper was given the necessary equipment and a list of 2,000 names with telephone numbers. This way, overall half the target population was contacted, representing ten million American homes.

This was the first time a single message was communicated in one given context using the same structure to so many people. The key to the success of this campaign is to be found in the extremely tight organisation of the 20,000 people who were made to work as a team. Political telemarketing was born.

In the following years the same type of campaigns were set up for Johnson, Humphrey, McGovern, Ford, Bob Kennedy and Reagan. Both the Democratic and Republican parties are now well aware of these techniques, both for raising funds and for promoting candidates.

Developments in France

It is practically impossible to call all the homes in a town or in a country during a telemarketing campaign organised to obtain votes. A selection must be made from the overall database by careful segmentation. It is not useful to contact people who are already in favour of the candidate, or who are extremely hostile to them. It is more cost-effective to work in the neutral zone, that is, among the undecided population.

In my experience, in any election it is possible to eliminate half the voters from any telemarketing action and ensure 90 per cent efficiency of operations. Analysing the populations of areas that can be thought the most advantageous is the first of the determining factors for political telemarketing. The second major contributing factor is the message. The pre-recorded telemessage technique on out-going phoning has the advantage of credibility (98 per cent of people will listen to the message) and of effectiveness in using helpers who are not trained in the professional skills of phoning.

The overall effectiveness of the campaign will depend on how well an appropriate script has been put together so as to work with an appropriate pre-recorded message. Voters' questions must be anticipated and an adequate answer should be prepared for each question. This answer must be part of the script which the helpers must never vary, so as to keep in line with the candidate's programme.

The third essential item for successful political telemarketing is to provide the team of supporters who will be making the phone calls with appropriate training. Operators must be selected who know how to listen to the voter. It is also necessary to set proper goals concerning the number of calls and the time spent on each call. For instance if a supporter has 1,000 leads to call he/she will only process 500 of those which will take up to 120 hours.

Organising supervision of the callers is the fourth key to success. It is essential to have a team of supervisors keeping tight account of the number of calls made every week by the supporters. This team of supervisors must have meetings with the phoning supporters in groups of ten at least once a week. If during the phoning campaign the phoners are operating part-time it is essential that the supervisors be working full-time.

A fifth factor of success is the follow-up to each call. It should not be forgotten that the telephone is being used to promote votes. It is a method of communication and not a tool for selling, as the voter does not sign up for anything. The favourable result of the contact will only show up on the date the vote is cast. It is therefore vital to have put as many chances as possible on your side by following up with a personalised letter sent to the voter and signed by the candidate. This mailshot must highlight the main points which the voter found important as discovered during the telephone call.

A dozen models of letters must have been prepared concerning the main points of interest for voters (employment, security, freedom, international affairs, health. . .); it will then be possible, with the help of a simple microcomputer connected to a printer, to mail from a centralised office, and using the telephone call sheets sent in by the phoners, the appropriate letter for each voter.

The letter the voter receives a few days after the telephone contact will create even more support: 'This candidate is really interested in me whereas her opponent is not taking any interest: he has not communicated with me at all, during the time she has phoned and written to me.'

This can make a big difference with the voters who will not have previously made a firm choice, as is the case with 40 per cent of voters in local elections and 20 per cent in the case of national elections.

PART II

SUCCESSFUL USES
OF TELEMARKETING

12

DIRECT SELLING

A must in telemarketing

Direct selling means closing a sales deal on the telephone. Direct selling can be done on out-going as well as on in-coming calls.

Although organising an in-coming call reception unit is more complicated than organising an out-going calling team, sales are much easier to close on in-coming phone calls.

If, for instance, a client of Marshall Cavendish calls one of the telephone bureaux to order a blouse she is paying for with her credit card, this sale has been made directly without intermediary. When, on behalf of a magazine, we call someone with a view to getting them to renew their subscription, when they agree this is a direct sale as they immediately receive the service without having to wait for their payment to be received.

With direct selling, the effect is immediate: phoners are able to quantify their sales, and work out their cost-effectiveness.

If three orders are obtained from ten calls made during one hour of phoning, you know whether the amount of sales generated makes the telemarketing approach cost-effective for each of the phoners and, which is more important, for the company that ordered the sales campaign. You then have the satisfaction of knowing that the telephone has really created the sales, which is not the case when a mailshot or a sales person's visit is necessary for closing.

Direct selling on the phone has to be done with the support of a written document, which may be a catalogue or a brochure, especially if you are targeting prospects outside your regular client list. When targeting clients, it is possible to sell on the phone without the help of any written material sent in before the call. However, this does depend on the bank's reputation and the products you are selling must be well-known.

It is true that bank representatives can make visits, but this is only cost-effective for major clients. Telemarketing is a particularly useful tool in the banking industry, as it allows contact with clients who have stopped visiting their branch, and who primarily rely on cash-machines for contact with their bank.

Direct selling in the banking industry is thought of as complementary sales or supplementary sales. By complementary or cross-selling, I mean selling new products to a client who is already using a specific product. By supplementary selling, we mean increasing the level of usage of a specific product by a client already using it.

Selling on in-coming phoning

Direct selling by phone originated with in-coming call campaigns generated by promoting a telephone number on written material.

Example
The 400 offices of the French company 'La Redoute' are spread over the whole of France. They have been making direct sales on in-coming calls for many years, 50 to 60 per cent of which will generate a sale. They make 50 per cent of their turnover on the phone. However, this did not happen easily.

In the 1970s, when 'La Redoute' attempted to launch direct selling on the phone during in-coming calls, the first results were quite negative. They advertised their phone number in their catalogue, but few calls were received.

At about that time, the management of 'La Redoute' contacted Murray Roman in New York to try to find out the reason for this failure. He made them understand that the launch of a new system of selling must, like any launch, be supported by an advertising campaign promoting the new service and creating client confidence. If clients are to use the phone, its usage must be sold to them before any other consideration is examined. Thus the advertising campaign, 'Dad calls La Redoute, Mum calls La Redoute' was launched.

As a result of this campaign, in-coming calling really took off. Successful selling on the telephone has to follow an important rule: when changing your methods, you must sell the means of communication before attempting to use the new system. Clients will not accept the idea of changing their habits of ordering without your having convinced them there are good reasons to do so.

Selling on an in-coming and out-going phoning mix

The main problem when setting up a team to process in-coming telephone calls is to match personnel and equipment to the volume of calls to be processed.

When a team of ten people is set up with a capability of processing 100 calls in an hour (ten per person), what happens if 110 calls are received in that hour or if 90 calls only are received? In the first case, your set-up is insufficient, in the second case the cost-effectiveness is poor.

Variations in volume of calls over each day and each week have to be provided for. Calls are always grouped during specific times of the day, yet your number of personnel cannot be modified from one hour to the next.

Recent technology has made it possible to improve the efficiency of systems for receiving in-coming calls, but the choices are the same for the organisation of personnel: you are either overstaffed or understaffed. The best answers are in supervising in-coming call operations and in developing out-going calling during the periods when in-coming calls are fewer. In this way it is possible to have a reserve of staff capable of processing peaks in the frequency of in-coming calls while using the staff on out-going calling on other campaigns or on client call-back. The part played by the supervisor is very important in switching staff from one mode to the other as the situation changes.

Example
Travel agents can process all in-coming calls and when the frequency of these is reduced, the staff can be used to call clients who have been put on a waiting list for a certain destination, to invite them to select another similar destination with the guarantee of a reservation.

Selling on out-going phoning

Direct selling on the phone can be done with total control of the organisation of calls and of the required staff. If you are using a list of 100,000 leads, knowing that each phoner will process ten leads per hour, you will know that 10,000 hours of out-going calling will be required. If a deadline has been fixed for completing the campaign, you know exactly what staffing is required. If you have one month to process the whole list, knowing that each phoner will work 100 hours in the month, you know you will need 100 phoners. If the campaign is given two months, you will only need half the number. In this type of operation it is easy to forecast the rhythm of work and the required means of production.

When his telephone rings, your client is not necessarily waiting for your call and every precaution must be taken to respect the consumer's private life and if necessary a call-back should be made later.

As the client has not initiated the call on an in-coming call, selling is more difficult. This is one of the reasons why the rules of the telemarketing profession preclude making direct selling calls to the homes of people who are not already clients of the calling company. This type of direct selling on out-going calls to unqualified prospects is absolutely not cost-effective. The rate of refusal is much too high to make the campaign worthwhile.

On the other hand, it is quite different when calling people who are already clients of or in contact with your company, especially when dealing with organisations for which the telephone is a usual tool of commercial communication.

Direct selling on out-going calls is usually cost-effective for the following:

- banking
- insurance
- newspapers
- office equipment
- car spare parts
- service industry.

In every case, you first need to develop a creative approach and to be aware of the profit margin.

Creative strategy

You should not assume that putting a good phoner in a telephone sales operation will set up your company for direct selling. A creative approach has to be found and this will need support from a direct selling professional. There are three elements which allow for creativity, as follows.

Qualifying prospects

You should target the prospect profile best adapted to direct selling. Large clients should be excluded.

The sales team engaged in face-to-face selling needs to be reassured. Direct selling on the phone will never replace an actual visit, but it can make cost-effective clients whose ordering does not justify a visit. The type of client to be addressed by direct selling campaigns on the telephone generally occupies the middle section of the pyramid of client population: those who make visiting a non cost-effective operation but who, on the whole, are sufficiently promising to justify systematic actions through a less costly method of communication.

Selecting and segmenting a client or prospect list is a key element in achieving success on the telephone.

The message

The message which is selected for the direct sales campaign requires a high degree of professional skills; phoners must not be left to their own devices with just a price list. The telephone script must be well-structured and follow a soft sale approach rather than a hard sale, as is sometimes done.

For instance, this is the wrong approach for a newspaper wishing to promote subscriptions. At the start of the telephone conversation they say: 'We have a particularly interesting offer to make for a two-year subscription at £63, instead of £98.96, which will save you 50 per cent on the normal price, or again a one-year subscription at £41.66 instead of £62.50 which is a 33 per cent saving. Would you prefer to save 50 per cent with a two-year subscription, or 33 per cent with a one-year subscription?' The right approach would be to say at the beginning of the call: 'Mr Jones, we are calling you to ask whether you would answer three questions:

1   In your experience, do you consider reading magazine X is difficult or enjoyable?
2   Do you consider the journalists on the staff of magazine X to be objective, partial or inconsistent?
3   In your opinion, does magazine X provide its readers with

original views and knowledge or does it just report information available everywhere?

The phoner must encourage the client to enlarge on their response. Following this opening, if the client's attitude has been more or less positive you are in a position to make an offer, and if not it is useless to go any further.

The structure

The third element of creativity in direct selling by phone concerns the organisation of the telephone system.

A telemarketing service never operates exclusively on out-going calling as certain clients will be calling back. On the other hand, an in-coming phoning activity alone is unsatisfactory without improving cost-effectiveness by combining it with out-going calls. This combination requires an appropriate structuring of staff.

This is best done with the use of computers, to enable operators to run a system in real time, so that the past history of each contact with every client is available at the time of the call. In the long run, this service will have to be run in-house, even if during the first tests operations are subcontracted to a third-party service company.

I have set up telemarketing services at Nixdorf, Bourjois, Peugeot Spare Parts, La Redoute, Firestone and Crédit Lyonnais, among others, and I know that such operations should be set up in-house and require training and organisation.

Telemarketing staff must be selected according to a very well-defined profile. It is not possible just to recycle existing personnel and to expect that effectiveness will just happen.

The first quality required of phoners is a feeling for communication, accompanied with a desire to serve the client. The second quality is the capacity to close a sale. The third quality is staying power which allows the phoner to go through the conversation for the twentieth time that day as though it were the first.

Five basic items have to be addressed when organising a telemarketing service:

- telephone installation and computerisation
- computer software
- selection and training of a supervisor
- selection and training of phoners
- daily monitoring of resulting ratios and figures.

Payment terms

Telemarketing sales have the advantage of avoiding intermediaries and offering comfortable margins. However, the system of payment conditions the success of operations.

When targeting telemarketing actions towards private individuals, the bank credit card is the system for the future. Certain companies have seen this so clearly they have created their own credit cards. Some consumers either do not have a bank card or do not wish to use it, preferring to pay on delivery of the goods, even if this means an extra cost. Whatever the payment terms, there may be problems when dealing with new customers but there should be no difficulties when dealing with clients whose paying habits are known.

In the case of banks or financial institutions, such as Diners Club or Amex, or any organisation such as Marks and Spencer who issues credit cards, automatic debit after issuing the monthly statement of invoices gives complete security.

In the case of business clients, payment is facilitated by the credibility enjoyed by companies, and this makes the distinction between new prospects and existing clients less sensitive. In every case, it is important that the invoicing and recovery of payment be fast and efficient so as to avoid any problems.

A company launching direct selling operations targeted at small- and medium-sized companies must not use the same payment terms as those applied to large and regular customers. Certain large companies who neglected this aspect met with considerable problems when client invoices increased in number from 1000 to 10,000 over a few weeks.

Telesales requires not only a good commercial organisation, but a good financial and accounts organisation. If your company publishes and distributes 500,000 copies of a catalogue and if during each call received you have to enquire whether your caller has an account with you, your accountancy methods are not up to handling your commercial strategy. Obtaining large profit margins by selling without intermediaries does not happen without a complete modification in the management of accounts.

Some outstanding successes

To summarise the principles, major European successes in recent years in each area of activity were the following:

The management of Newsweek shows a readiness to use the newest techniques. Newsweek operates an internal telesales unit for their catalogue, which processes direct sales of the products listed in the catalogue.

Barclays Bank, the BNP in France, and Midland Bank are very active in telesales. Barclays are highly adaptable and in a position to take immediate advantage of any new technique. This is of vital importance because large companies often have a cumbersome internal structure which makes it difficult to set up an activity like telesales, which affects the services department for the telephone, data processing for specialised software, training departments for integrating operations, logistics for the general organisation and the sales department for the actual operation, which naturally slows down implementation of a telesales or other new campaign.

In selling direct to other businesses, Xerox, IBM Direct, Mémorex and Inmac pioneered the promotion of office equipment. As customers' use of their products grows, these companies are in a position to sell them products of increasing value (terminals, printers). These are add-on sales as defined in those industries.

In industry, suppliers of equipment have now perceived the extraordinary potential provided by telesales. Peugeot sell on the phone to their 450 dealers who are regularly called by a team of specialist phoners operating on a daily basis; dealers will in turn call retailers and garage operators to promote offers of spare parts. This system multiplies the sales people communicating to the widest possible target.

13

PROSPECTING FOR CUSTOMERS

Increasing productivity

Telephone researching for leads increases productivity in the sales field, by providing sales teams anywhere in the world with considerable value from the information they collect. Instead of wasting time on useless contacts, the field sales person will concentrate on the 'hot' prospects selected through telemarketing. The sales person's productivity is considerably increased as he/she will be meeting only people who have shown an interest in the product.

Telemarketing makes it possible to detect out of any 1,000 companies the 80 companies which have a data processing project. These 80 leads passed on to the technical sales people in Bull or IBM do not mean contracts are ready and automatic. The sales person's work still has to be done to demonstrate that his or her brand is the best.

In the last five years, IBM has set up telemarketing centres in Europe designed to locate from lists of tens of thousands of small- and medium-sized companies, those having data processing projects and thus those who would be interested in IBM's products. In France, for example, 10,000 good leads are passed on to the IBM field sales team each year.

The telemarketing system set up by IBM was initiated in the United States with the help of Murray Roman and Michael Violanti. Large American multinational companies have often been the first to set up large telemarketing centres in Europe with the support of information or strategic recommendations from the United States. This was also the case for Xerox in the UK who, in 1978, organised a client prospecting system which had been successful in the United States from 1974 onwards and which covered all areas of the British Isles.

Michael Violanti, acting as a consultant to Rank Xerox UK at that time, spent six months in London setting up twenty telemarketing centres. In the same way, 3M, Kodak, Monsanto, Avis and Hertz used the experience of their mother companies in the United States to set up European telemarketing centres. European groups in turn, having witnessed the successful launch of such operations by American subsidiaries, decided to follow suit. For example, large French companies such as Peugeot, and Citroën, focused on using telemarketing as a means of communicating with clients.

Any company selling equipment or services through a team of field sales people is increasingly aware of the considerable improvements in productivity which are to be obtained by the use of the telephone to supply the sales force with leads. A sales person selling face-to-face spends on average only 30 per cent of her time in client interviews, so the possibility of increasing that percentage from 30 to 40 per cent using the support of telemarketing is enough to tempt any company director.

The 1 + 1 = 3 rule

When applying telemarketing to the prospecting of potential clients, success depends to a considerable extent on good coordination between the telemarketing team preparing the contact and the sales team who follow up. As with all problems of coordination, it is the management's job to create this positive relationship. The telephone must fit in closely with face-to-face selling actions to ensure a good balance and good results.

I have witnessed excellent telemarketing campaigns which produced poor results because the sales team was not following up the information passed on, which was not even looked at. I have known telemarketing campaigns of average quality which gave acceptable results because the sales team processed appropriately the leads obtained, even if there was not an abundance of them.

How do you ensure the best possible coordination between the phone team and the sales team in the field? That is the most important question which a manager in charge of a face-to-face selling team should answer before launching into any telemarketing action.

The first thing that will help is to ensure that the sales team experience the work of the telemarketing team so they understand all aspects of that activity. A telephone training session of the field sales team using the phoners' scripts will help with the integration of the method. After having experienced one day of the conditions under which the phoners work, the face-to-face sales person will understand the quality of the leads obtained. He or she will also understand that it is a specialised job which should be left to specially trained people. The credibility of telemarketing will be improved and there will not be a feeling that the phoner is taking the place of the field sales person to close deals.

The second element for good coordination is to organise the phoners' operations so they are in close contact with the sales team without establishing any hierarchical levels between them, but with the head of sales supervising interactions between these two types of specialists. We recommend that the workplace of the telemarketing team, if it is not in the same offices as the field sales team's office, be nearby so that meetings can be organised at least twice a month.

The third element facilitating integration is to stimulate interest on the part of the sales team for the launch of telemarketing operations by giving them a special premium on each sale obtained from a lead obtained from the phoner. It is important and natural that each time a sales person closes a contract they have the feeling that it is their creation. The product itself, the promotion and telemarketing operation, are perceived as being supports, while the client is very much perceived as 'my client'. This attitude is natural and there is no reason to go against it as long as the client's cheque is paid to the company.

It must be acknowledged that sales people sell better. It is important, however, to establish a balance in attitudes when it is a mix of means which has created success. After a few months the sales people will have been convinced of the efficiency of the support they receive from the phoning operation, as their normal commission will have increased.

The creative approach

The script used when phoning to locate potential buyers who are then given to the sales team as leads must always be vetted by the head of sales and by the field sales team. Writing such a script requires a different creative approach to writing selling scripts. The objective is not to close on the phone, but to get the prospect talking and to acquire information. It is journalistic or detective work. Prospects must feel at ease so that they can communicate their problems and the level of answers they are considering.

Prospect-screening scripts should be written in four steps:

- questions about situations
- questions about dissatisfactions
- questions about intentions
- questions about answers.

Questions about situations will serve to analyse the activity, the habits, the product or the service, the financing methods or any other information relating to the prospect that will help in establishing a profile.

Questions concerning areas of dissatisfaction will reveal explicitly or implicitly an underlying dissatisfaction. For example, no one will admit to having bought a bad car, so a prospect will never, except in very serious cases, express dissatisfaction explicitly. This would be admitting that he/she made a bad choice. The blunt question 'Are you satisfied with your car after having driven 50,000 miles?' is badly put, as 95 per cent of prospects will answer 'Yes'.

Questions concerning dissatisfactions must be put carefully, insisting on specific points. 'Concerning the cost of after-sale services, do you think X (giving the name of the brand owned by the prospect) offers reasonable costs for repairs?' 'Are you quite satisfied with the services given by your dealer and the contacts you have had with the sales people?' 'Is there any detail on which you are dissatisfied with your interaction with the brand, the dealer, the repairs shop, etc.?' Creativity plays an important part when formulating such questions.

The same rule applies to questions concerning intentions and solutions, and the telephone has a specific advantage in making it possible to test easily each formulation and arrive at truthful answers.

A good telephone script for qualifying prospects must be tested on 150 to 200 calls before it is considered satisfactory. It is important to distinguish between 'market surveys' and 'detecting buyers'. If you wish to develop your sales or if you are simply obtaining information on a market, scripts will be different. Certain companies build scripts for detecting buying intentions which will include 40 questions, of which 35 are situation questions.

This type of approach does not serve to detect buyers, for two reasons. First, the prospect interviewed soon feels harassed, so stops being objective as a potential buyer, which creates confusion between a potential need and a real project. Second, the cost of each contact may become prohibitive when the sales results of the campaign are compared with the costs of the telemarketing action. Between a five-minute contact, which is the average for calls made to detect buyers, and a fifteen-minute contact, which is the average for market research calls, there will be an increase in cost of three to four times. This extra cost will not be acceptable to analysis of campaign cost-effectiveness.

Out-going or in-coming

Detection of buyers can be carried out by out-going phoning as well as on in-coming calls. The script used with a view to qualify the degree of interest shown by the in-coming caller must resemble the script created for out-going phoning.

It is, however, extremely important for maximum efficiency to ask an in-coming caller the details concerning their name, address and phone number. This information will make it possible to have, right from the start, an idea of the caller's profile and degree of interest. Without detailed information concerning the caller, the sales team will not give the lead any credibility. Either they will follow up and might meet someone who is just inquisitive, or a company without the necessary means, or they will do nothing because they will not feel sufficiently secure in the context of the lead.

Example
After an advertising campaign in the media promoting a freephone number, IBM invited people who rang to come and see the operation of

the personal computer they were marketing. The company who processed the calls for IBM received about 10,000 calls which they failed to qualify. During the first demos given on the PC, IBM managers realised that 80 per cent of visitors coming to the IBM centres were individuals who would never invest the necessary amount in a personal microcomputer. If the company processing the calls had qualified the prospects, IBM sales people would not have wasted their time over the weeks.

The golden rule with answering in-coming calls is to establish the quality of leads by careful processing before they are passed on to the sales team.

It is also possible to work efficiently in two stages, as follows:

– accepting calls and just taking basic prospect information
– calling prospects back using the information obtained on the in-coming call and qualifying the lead.

Use this method when the pressure of in-coming calls makes it difficult to qualify callers carefully. It is then preferable to call the prospect back both to show consideration and to qualify their need, before passing the lead on to the sales force. This method is particularly worth using when, after an advertising campaign on television, in-coming calls are coming in over a very short period of time. In such cases, phoners must obtain the basic information within one minute so as to create a list for calling back the next day for proper qualification.

There are cases of in-coming calls coming in at a rate of 10,000 calls in 30 minutes, which was more than could be properly processed, even for recording basic information. In such cases, qualification of callers took place at a later stage on out-going calling.

Freephone numbers are going to be used more and more frequently as a feature of television advertising campaigns for vehicle products, financial products, or home equipment.

You may use an advertising agency which has the necessary television experience; however, the input of telemarketing professionals is important if you wish to follow up people who are responding to a TV spot and who are calling for more information or to place an order. Success depends on the information which is passed on to the sales people; coordination between the TV campaign and the telesales campaign; an accurate choice of channels and time slots; effective follow-up. Cost-effectiveness, not only of the information passed on but of the signed order, should be considered at all times.

If we take the case of the automobile industry, success depends on five major factors:

- choice of the offer
- an appropriate message for that offer
- choice of the TV support environment and the time slot
- qualification of in-coming callers' intentions
- dynamising the sales team for follow-up actions.

Using data processing

If you wish to maximise the benefits obtained from using the phone, you will have to use data processing to manage the information you collect. This is what Americans call data-based marketing. The information bank or database is the heart of all prospecting activities in your company.

Telemarketing allows you to detect immediate prospective buyers, but the information collected concerning other prospects who will be in the market in the medium- or long-term should not be neglected. The telephone makes it possible for you to assess 'hot prospects' to be followed up immediately through your sales force, 'warm prospects' will have to be followed up through marketing actions at a later date, and 'cold prospects', on whom you need not waste time. The volume of information collected must be integrated into a computerised management system of various levels of sophistication.

Data processing can be used simply for storing information or with a system like Profit Tool, for instance, which is a high power software package that can process data around five features:

- automatic printing out of call-back
- real-time processing of information
- immediate analysis of various coefficients to assess each prospect's value
- immediate calculation of phoners' performance
- obtaining statistical information for segmenting lists.

Profit Tool allows the marketing department of a company not only to have knowledge of buyers of computer hardware but also to establish very accurate statistics concerning users' dissatisfactions, for example, with competitor products in each type of industry, for each competitor brand in each geographical area, and for each job position within the user company. These elements are an extremely useful aid to decision-making. Profit Tool operates in real time so for some companies, eg. Bull, phoners have VDUs on which the phoning script is displayed as necessary and phoners enter data as it is collected, while for others, eg. IBM, phoners do not capture data in real time but send hard copy leads to a specialised data capture bureau. In both cases, the database is built up from the telephone plus data processing combination.

Real-time data-entry does not increase productivity sufficiently to make it a necessary choice when you are telemarketing simply to qualify prospects. The productivity gain just about balances the extra cost. However, companies dedicated to data processing may wish to work in real time as it conforms to their culture.

Real-time telemarketing work is, however, necessary when historical data concerning a client or a prospect needs to be accessed during the call, in particular on in-coming calls. For instance, when a client calls Xerox for the telesales service, the phoner consults his or her workstation to discover the client profile, any special client terms, etc. On out-going calling, as the call is made at your own initiative, the lead's call-sheet should give the phoner all the information needed.

At the present time, there are strong differences of opinion concerning, not the principle of data processing in telemarketing operations, but as to whether real-time data capture or batch data capture are the best solutions. My personal experience would be to recommend real-time operation for in-coming calling and batch data capture for out-going campaigns. Telemarketing out-going campaigns require the support of a whole team of data processing specialists on an on-going basis if phoners are working on VDU workstations. In cases where 100,000 calls have to be processed, the types of problems which should make you hesitate to use real-time data processing. In this field, choices must be made around optimising cost-effectiveness and not around the aesthetic aspect of operations. However, each case should be analysed in depth before a decision is made.

Using electronic mail

The single item most likely to be a support to telemarketing in the coming years is electronic mail. This tool is a reliable solution to the problem of centralisation. For many years decentralisation of telemarketing operations has been recommended by setting up units in the various branches of large groups as well as in dealerships or distributing agents. The main objective of this strategy was to establish close coordination with the field sales force, we have already discussed. Achieving close contact between the sales people and the phoners ensures the $1 + 1 = 3$ synergy. In some cases, however, for instance in a vehicle dealership, one phoner served three or four sales people, with the result that the phoner worked in a very solitary environment.

Electronic mail now makes it possible to centralise phoners' teams under the supervision of a telephone specialist in a given site. Without this coordination communication with the dispersed field sales people is impossible. With the Minitel network, for instance, it is possible to pass on every day the hot prospects to the sales people so that follow-up is carried out efficiently. This overcomes the disadvantage of centralising. The disadvantage of a non-supervised, decentralised phoning operation is also removed. Electronic mail therefore provides new answers.

Experience shows that decentralising phoners' operations so that there is a local shortage of expertise and creativity is not efficient. Centralising operations and expertise, if no fast communication system is available with the teams ensuring follow-up in the field, is also not a good solution. It is easier to use electronic mail to communicate information than to decentralise supervision and creativity. Training dispersed teams in the skills of telemarketing, the analysis of targets, the creation of strategies, and the writing of scripts, is difficult to achieve and can only be done over a few years. The best solution is to use electronic mail tools to send out information on 'hot prospects' to the sales team, obtained with a centralised telemarketing team of phoners properly supervised.

A noteworthy success

The most successful telemarketing operations for the detection of potential buyers are not the campaigns run over a short period, but the on-going campaigns, as the qualification of prospects needs frequent telemarketing call-backs. Running through the list of prospects two or three times a year is necessary to obtain the maximum quality from a telemarketing operation aimed at screening prospects.

Companies which have set up on-going in-house telemarketing operations are more successful in this field than those which have just attempted short-lived operations to solve a given problem, instead of aiming at creating interesting leads on an on-going basis for their field sales team.

The example of Atlas Copco in 1981 is typical. The French subsidiary of this Swedish multinational was facing two problems. First, it had no information on the buyers of compressors and other compressed-air equipment. Second, the company was selling its product through non-exclusive outlets which were rather passive in the market.

The objective was to dynamise dealers by supplying them with information on existing buying intentions in their area. Atlas Copco asked Phone Marketing to develop an efficient strategy to penetrate the market. In an initial stage, we applied a test to four selected dealerships out of 1,500 existing dealers. This test gave very good results for two of the dealerships and poor results for the two others. When such a variation occurs, you know that telemarketing has been successful in the qualification of prospects, but that there is a definite problem in the sales team's follow-up operation. When these follow-up operations were analysed, we realised that in one of the dealerships with poor results there were no out-going field sales people, and in the case of the second a head of sales was reluctant to accept any interference in his operations.

As a result of this test, Atlas Copco decided to use systematic telemarketing. Using a list of 30,000 selected small- and medium-sized industries, we organised a screening operation on the phone which allowed us to create a database of 20,000 companies. A team of five phoners was specially trained on a script developed during the initial test to make a first general call to all the companies in the database. It took six months for the phoners' team to call the whole of the list at the rate of five useful contacts per hour and per phoner. At the end of six months, the whole list was called again to update the information.

Out of the list of 20,000 companies, each calling campaign identified 1,400 to 1,500 leads which deserved to be followed up by the dealers. Out of 14,000 leads followed up, one out of three generated a sale of, on average, £20,000. Telemarketing costs were less than £200 per sale. At the end of three years, the management of Atlas Copco made an extremely interesting analysis; the dealerships who had joined the telemarketing scheme had increased their sales by the ratio of 1:2.9 for that type of equipment. Dealers who had not joined the scheme had increased their sales for the same equipment by the ratio of 1:1.2. Atlas Copco then extended this system to all other European countries.

14

SURVEYS AND RESEARCH

Marketing and cost-effectiveness objectives

Surveys need a different approach from the traditional telephone approach, in as much as the objective is not immediate cost-effectiveness, but gathering qualitative information. The marketing department of a large company is usually very structured, and usually has a research division in charge of market analysis, products and development.

In the past, surveys and studies were often sub-contracted to traditional specialist polling companies such as Louis Harris or Burke. Staffed by teams of expert face-to-face interviewers, these companies used to perform a large number of surveys. However, they are less likely to undertake such surveys today for two reasons. First, large companies have themselves learned to write scripts and implement studies, so consequently only the actual interviewing is sub-contracted. Second, traditional specialist companies are not able to carry out large telephone operations at a cost which is competitive compared with telemarketing companies.

It is therefore important to invest in the recruitment of talented executives, in order to bring real competence in the conception, the implementation and the analysis of the studies. Expertise is required in the planning and implementation of the following three areas:

- study of the concept (preparing and testing the script)
- implementation (carrying out face-to-face, phone or written questionnaires)
- analysis of results.

Usually, polling organisations are competent in these areas, but are weak on telemarketing approaches. Telemarketing companies, on the contrary, are not usually so competent in these three areas.

The telephone is increasingly used in preference to face-to-face interviews for reasons of cost. Phone surveys are usually five times cheaper than face-to-face surveys. In the future the telephone should increase its market share in the studies and surveys market, especially for quantitative studies. The telephone is essential for quantitative surveys carried out on more than 2,000 interviewees.

Types of surveys suited to the phone

Clearly, quantitative studies with more than forty questions are usually badly adapted to the phone and need to be done through face-to-face interviews. The telephone is best suited to studies with fewer than fifteen questions and fewer than 1,000 persons to interview. For example, a survey carried out by telephone of 50,000 interviews would cost close to £2 million. The cost of an equivalent face-to-face study would be about £15 million.

Apart from price and service, competitive advantages for companies, both nationally and abroad, are not determining factors for modern companies. In the long run, price wars result in an erosion of profit margins and consequently of investments. This represents a danger for the survival of the company. Service is therefore the surest way to make a difference to the client, and customer care is an increasingly important pre-occupation of large enterprises. However, the concept of quality of service is difficult to measure unless you use repeated polls, which can offer a barometer of the effectiveness of your services. In order to be significant, these studies, especially for consumer markets, have to address all points of sale and therefore require you to contact a great number of clients.

Tabulating the results of the calls allows you to focus the targeting during the campaign in order to validate the polls. Information technology (IT) can play an important role in large studies, as it avoids the necessity of proof reading and data capture. There are several successful software packages which work quite well with small samples (less than 2,000).

The main problem with polling large numbers of people is

quality control at the level of the operator. Certain studies, in order to avoid bias, require changing interviewers after 100 interviews. During the study, it is important to plan adequate supervision. A good ratio is one supervisor for five to ten telephoners. The supervisor has to be very active in listening in to the conversation, recording client queries, and analysing productivity ratios per hour.

15

ATTRACTING CUSTOMERS TO YOUR SALES CENTRE

Making your sales office cost-effective

Many companies invest large sums of money in setting up their client reception areas. If only ten potential clients visit these facilities in one day, their efforts do not generate much return. Maximising the number of clients visiting sales centres or showrooms is the major preoccupation of all company managers who want to make their space cost-effective.

In the car industry, banking, housing development, or distribution, increasing the number of visits influences directly the level of sales. In industry, company managers know that the number of sales is directly linked to the number of demonstrations conducted.

In that context, telemarketing has had a very favourable reception for two reasons. First, it allows you to select your visitors in order to avoid wasting time. Second, it allows you to bring in potential clients in numbers suited to your sales capacity. Indeed, the most common problem with traditional promotional operations designed to increase traffic in your sales area rests in the number of contacts your sales force has to handle. For example, during operations called 'Open doors in the vehicle industry', over a three-day period, the dealership may have to handle up to 1,000 people; this might be damaging to the effectiveness of the sales force who will not know who to respond to. Over one hour, six or seven sales people cannot communicate with 100 people. The telephone, however, allows you to monitor and regulate the rhythm of visits in accordance with your space and available resources.

Generating useful activity

Telemarketing is a means of selecting each visitor, by asking questions prior to their visit to the centre about their buying projects, their habits, or their objectives. There are ways other than the telephone to create traffic at a dealership, but telemarketing is an effective back-up method.

Example

Citroën sent out a mailing designed to produce traffic at their dealerships. The mailing included a cheque for £500 that could be used towards the purchase of a Citroën, and also included a guarantee of trade-in on their old vehicle at market value. Initially, the offer was valid for a limited period.

After the first mailing Citroën managed to obtain a level of 4 to 6 per cent of people coming in to the dealership. On average, one sale was generated per four visitors. Following that effort, Citroën central sales office used the telephone to follow up the same type of mailing. In that instance the level of visits was 18 per cent overall and the conversion rate was 20 per cent. Obviously Citroën continued the approach, and varied the offers because their competitors attempted to trivialise the offer in the eyes of the consumer.

This example demonstrates the importance of telemarketing and direct mail in general to select visitors at your point of sale.

Day-to-day activity

As any company has daily expenses, it must have daily income. Creating traffic at the sales centre should not be like a three-day bout of feverish activity followed by three months of inactivity. The ideal situation is to create an even flow of people that is commensurate with your resources. If your sales team can deal with twenty clients per day, the ideal level would be to create twenty visits per working day of the month. Telemarketing is the only way to end up with a balance. For example, if we know that calling 100 people a day will generate twenty visits, this means that a monthly programme of 2,000 calls will allow you to optimise traffic at your sales centre. The company will therefore be able to survive day-to-day and will be less subject to publicity stunts.

This strategy explains why some distributors have integrated a permanent telemarketing team in order to ensure a daily traffic at their sales centre. They have performed the necessary tests and have found the mathematical correlation. The basic question is: 'How many prospects do I have to phone in order to generate the number of visits that is matched to my daily capacity?' Under consistent conditions, telemarketing can produce a consistent level of response. The results are mathematically reliable, which will reassure the manager. However, the system must constantly be improved in order to fight competition and to keep pace with the evolution of the market.

Example

IBM's demonstration seminar example is noteworthy. Out of 100 people called, between fifteen and twenty say they will come to the seminar; the number who show up varies between ten and fifteen. Three to four IBM sales people attend each demo, and this allows one sales person to manage three potential clients.

Media strategies

Quite often, distributors do not have a database of prospects. In order to generate potential buyers, it is essential to communicate by print, radio and television through a direct response mechanism. Direct response requires the prospect's willingness to ask for information. In these cases an 0800 number or a response card is made available to generate responses. Each response is handled through telemarketing. Each respondent is qualified if that is part of the strategy, and then referred to the dealer and followed up.

The aim of this approach, apart from to build a database, is to generate demand on the part of the consumer and redirect this national demand on to a local distributor. For example, in housing development – where it is very difficult to build databases – a sequence of television plus telephone, or radio plus telephone, generates leads of prospects interested in buying a house. These leads can then be referred to the sales people.

However, success is dependent on the sales force's conversion ability. As we have seen in previous chapters, this is an essential element of telemarketing success. However, if there is a lack of psychological preparation within the sales force or the dealerships, contacts established by telephone are not always converted properly into customers.

This system is rapidly developing in the UK, in France and in Germany. In the UK there are more and more television commercials with 0800 numbers.

Working with electronic mail

One major problem that occurs when following up contacts generated by telephone is passing these contacts over to dealers. When you must coordinate several hundred dealers, electronic mail is an important tool. Using a specially designed electronic mail programme, contacts generated through telemarketing can be data captured and sorted by distributor code on the computer.

Using a diary system – a minitel system – which identifies opening days, the dealer can look at the daily appointments arranged through telemarketing. These appointments may have been generated through a sequence of out-going telephone marketing followed by a media campaign, followed by an in-coming operation.

In either case, the names of potential clients must be handed over to dealers with maximum efficiency by electronic mail. Dealers must consult their minitel every day in order to follow up clients. The central computer has to have enough communication lines to maximise the use of the minitel and not create any backlog. For example, for 300 dealers the minimum number of lines needed is 100. Updates on these contacts can be made on this system, and statistical analysis carried out.

Apart from electronic mail, other communication procedures such as telex, the post, fax or telephone have their problems when used to pass information on to dealers. Telex cannot be used to communicate different messages to 300 distributors, the post is slow and unreliable, and faxes cannot be used on a large scale. It is difficult, except in emergencies, to communicate long messages with fifteen or more names a day through the telephone to 300 distributors.

However, electronic mail is best avoided when there is a small number of contacts to communicate. When transmitting ten contacts to a distributor over a two-week period, the system has drawbacks. A dealer using the minitel system twice in a row without getting any contacts will not be inclined to use it again.

Example

During the Peugeot 405 launch, Automobile Peugeot wanted to generate visits at their dealerships. They wanted to introduce the new model to their existing clients before the public launch. It was a positive move on Peugeot's part to think of their clients first and give them preferential treatment. It meant handling a database with 200,000 individuals who had to be directed to 450 dealers. Telemarketing was chosen as a communication support. Over a ten-day period, a team of 200 telephoners had to direct these clients to an appropriate dealer.

The names of clients interested in this preview were data captured and assigned to the relevant dealer, who used minitel to check the appointments made for him/her.

Out of the original list of 200,000 clients, 100,000 were contacted by phone and 30,000 agreed to visit dealers. Out of these 30,000 clients, 20,000 visited dealers during the preview period.

This was the largest 'telemarketing plus electronic mail' campaign run in France. It included the largest number of dealers and the largest database of clients. Without electronic mail, this campaign would have been impossible to run. It followed all the conditions for success in telemarketing, where the objective was to generate visits; namely, these were qualified visits, well-organised, and at a frequency the dealers could handle effectively.

16

ORGANISING TELEPHONING WITHIN THE COMPANY

Analysing lost calls

- A large company loses an incredible number of clients because 30 per cent of incoming calls remain unanswered by the sales department. On Friday afternoons it is practically impossible to contact the sales force.
- In a large multinational market leader, it can take up to 30 minutes to obtain sales information.

How many people are prepared to wait that long before calling competitors? A recent study showed that telephone skills were neglected in more than 70 per cent of companies. The concept of 'future client on the line' is completely underestimated.

One French company, Phone Marketing, aware of these problems, has set up an analysis system of communications on the phone both within a company and at the switchboard level. Their objective is to diagnose the quality of phone reception skills at all levels. The analysis is precise and recommendations are given to improve these skills.

They work with three objectives as follows:

- to measure and control the quality of reception at the switchboard and at the secretarial level
- to establish a complete diagnosis of the use of the telephone throughout the company
- to make recommendations in order for the company to derive maximum efficiency from their telephone reception efforts.

Programme concept

The work they do rests on a number of contacts made by them within the company being audited. These contacts are adapted according to criteria relevant to the size, the structure and the locality of divisions, Head Office and subsidiaries within the company.

Duration: the normal duration of an audit corresponds to a two-week period of continuous calling, in other words, ten working days.

Time slots: these calls are run throughout the day according to two schedules, which allow Phone Marketing to test at each period of the day the telephone reception behaviour of the company, as follows:

- Priority hours or normal working hours: 9.00 am to 1 pm and 2.30 to 5.30 pm.
- Peak hours: 8.30 to 9.00 am – 12 to 2.30 pm – 5.30 to 7.00 pm.

Call scenarios: it is essential, in order to be credible, that the test calls resemble those the company receives every day. The situations the mock callers use depend on the type of company. They can be targeted to the switchboard, to one of several divisions, or to all the company's divisions. Generally, these situations are as follows:

- looking for an individual
- looking for a skill
- sales enquiry
- administrative or accounting query
- general information
- potential supplier
- sales call
- personal call
- press call.

Measurement criteria: Each call is measured using qualitative and quantitative factors.

Qualitative factors:

- introduction
- dialogue quality
- quality of the information given
- quality of the music on hold, if used

- how well the message was understood
- filtering process
- orientation process.

Quantitative factors:

- waiting time before call was picked up
- duration of the call (between pick up by reception and hand over)
- percentage of unfulfilled calls
- number and frequency of the return on the line (in case of hold).

Methodology

Whatever the audit's features or its scope, the procedure is as follows:

1 Phone Marketing specialists draw up a organisation check-list (call-frequency chart, implementation plan, rating grid, staff rotation schedule, control and follow-up, analysis of results and trends).
2 The Account Manager writes the different scenarios depending on the situations to be studied.
3 The Account Manager trains the telephoners.
4 Under the Account Manager the phoners implement the calls which are made according to the telephone grid period. The latter is conceived according to the duration of the study in such a way that all scenarios are spread out throughout all time slots.

   This grid highlights the number and destination of each call and allows, through a rotation system, changing people according to the situation.

   For each call, a score card is drawn up and a duplicate is given to the client. This score card highlights the telephone image, the handling of calls, and any useful comment.
5 As well as the score cards, a comprehensive report is also given at the end of the study.

Analysis

This is the most important part of the study in as much as its objective is to diagnose the use of the telephone and also allow suggestions for additional training in order to maximise efficiency. All call sheets are converted to score cards which are analysed according to three factors:

- standards and scenarios (divisions studied, number of calls received for each scenario, comments)
- tally of reactions (high points and low points at switchboard and secretary levels)
- recommendations to improve the quality of the reception and optimise the effectiveness of the response.

At the end of the analysis, a global summary is given which is illustrated with samples of conversations. At the end of the audit, Phone Marketing can set up a training programme that can be implemented immediately.

The 'expansion bomb' effect

In July 1987, Phone Marketing published in a French journal a report on the quality of phone receptions in major French groups. This report had a dramatic effect in large French companies since it found that in more than 20 per cent of cases an individual cannot get through to the company. This is what Roger Alexandre, a journalist on the journal wrote:

Companies, beware of Alexander Graham Bell. Certain managers still imagine that this man's invention is only used for long distance calls. A bad mistake. Above all, the telephone is a great revealer. An undercover spy. A soul searcher. It is through the telephone that the first contact between the company and most of its contacts is made. Just a 'clic' and an ear is plugged in, plunged within the company, ready to discover a multitude of essential facts about it, such as its efficiency, quality consciousness, the motivation of its staff, etc. . . . . Well, let it be known: your image starts at the switchboard.

A few managers got the message in a painful way. For example, the head of a French National Bank was phoned by his wife one day and when she asked for him at the switchboard she heard at the end of the line perplexity, ruffled pages, and then 'I'm sorry, madam, we have nobody here by that name'. The puzzled wife said that she was calling the President of the bank. 'Oh, no,' she was told, 'the President's name on the information sheet is . . .', and she was given the name of his predecessor who had been fired six months previously.

The results of Phone Marketing's work show that proper use of the telephone is not very widespread in companies. Out of 72 companies studied, only eight scored between 16 and 18, nine scored between 10 and 12, and five go below the mean.

Companies in distribution and information technology seem to have the best telephone reception skills: Les Nouvelles Galeries, La Redoute, Bull, IBM. At the other end of the list are: Michelin, Usinor, Lesieur, L'Oréal, Rhône Poulenc, Pernod, Colgate, . . . At the end of this chapter is a list ranking the organisations studied by Phone Marketing.

One of the surprise findings was the large number of calls that never reached their destination: these represented 11.5 per cent of the total if one includes cases where the switchboard did not answer or was engaged, interrupted calls (at the switchboard or during the calls transfer), and including cases where testers gave up, discouraged after being on hold for twenty minutes. On this last point Michelin beat all records; 6 per cent of calls that they received ended in that way – in the silence of infinite space. At EDF, they practised guillotine telephone; as soon as you got through, 'click', you were cut off (16 per cent of all calls). The same problem was experienced at Philips (13 per cent), at l'UAP, at the Crédit Lyonnais, at CIC, Kodak, BIS and – again – Michelin. At CGE or Usinor, you didn't even get a chance to say hello before you were cut off!

FNAC and Général Motors were the champions of the continuously engaged switchboards, or never answering switchboards. In 40 per cent of cases there was no answer. The most credible explanation was that they have a considerable lack of telephone resources, but is the lack a result of foresight or stinginess? Also guilty of not answering were Usinor, Publicis, Club Méditerranée, l'UAP, Volkswagen, Air Inter, Peugeot and Diners Club.

The results of tests on how foreign languages were received gave pretty good results for large companies; 88 per cent of English calls were taken and handled, and 63 per cent of those in German. Some French receptionists did seem to be thrown by a German accent. Here is a call that was made to a distribution company:

'Ich möchte an Ihren Finanzdirektor einen Brief senden . . .
No, no, speak French! (*nervous operator*)
Ich möchte . . .
No, me not understand, speak French. (*operator in a panic*)
Ich möchte . . .

No, hand me over to somebody who speaks French. (*despairing operator*)
Fräulein, bitte . . .' (click)

In France, switchboards in public service companies showed themselves to be most adverse to Shakespeare and Goethe: only 67 per cent of calls in English and 12 per cent of calls in German were handled. But there were two companies where anyone who did not speak French nearly always got hung up on; EDF (Electricité de France) and Havas.

Overall, large companies had quite good telephone skills even though their operators appeared to finish their own conversation after picking up the phone (Air Inter, Procter & Gamble, CGE, Philips, Colgate) and even though on visiting the head office it was easy to get the feeling one was intruding. For example, this was a call to a large car manufacturer:

'Hello, I would like to know if you take back used cars.
Hold on . . . (followed by a fifteen-minute silence from the switchboard, then:) yes?
Ah, I was starting to get bored.
Look, madam, we are not glued to our seats.
I was calling to find out if you took back used vehicles?
Oh, no, you have to call a dealer.
I live in . . ., could you give me an address?
I don't know, but you can find one in the Yellow Pages.'

This is enough to throw anyone into the arms of the competition. Another noticeable feature was that reception became rather cool if calling about a job or if one was a supplier. Soliciting was not well received. For example, this conversation took place in a private heavy industry company:

'Hello, we are a business school and we are organising an evening at the end of June. We would like some financial help.
No, absolutely not, especially not for business schools, it's begging, what a dirty habit, Goodbye.' (Click)

Lovers of bizarre trivia will relish the time slots phenomenon. There were indeed some times when calls were better received than others. Overall, it was better to call in the afternoon especially in the car and consumer goods industries. But the opposite was true for service industries, who were more friendly in the morning.

Here are the results of the *L'Expansion* study of 72 companies (scores from 0 to 20):

The Best: over 18
Bull

The Very Good: 16 to 18
Carrefour
Iveco
Darty
IBM
Auchan
Canal Plus
ECCO

The Good Ones: 16 to 14
Moët-Hennessy
Thomson
Paribas
Accor
Nouvelles Galeries
La Redoute
Casino
Société Générale
Dassault
Trois Suisses
RSCG
L'Air Liquide
Kodak
RATP
CCF
Rank Xérox
Havas
Télécom
Renault
Péchiney
Apple
American Express
Elf
Digital

The Average: 12 to 14
BIS
CIC

Nestlé
Philips
Mercedes
TF1
BNP
Moulinex
Saint-Gobain
Citroën
Volkswagen
Crédit Lyonnais
CGE
BIC
Proctor & Gamble
Air France
EDG
Olivetti
Crédit Agricole
SNCF
Colgate
Drouot
Fiat
Diners Club
Pernod
Rhône Poulenc

The Mediocres: 10 to 12
Printemps
Peugeot
Air Inter
L'Oréal
Publicis
Antenne 2
Lesieur
Ford
Club Méditerranée

The Very Bad: 8 to 10
Usinor
Michelin
FNAC

The Worst: less than 8
Général Motors

Since this research was carried out a large number of these have definitely improved thanks to a comprehensive programme of telephone skills.

17

SECURING CLIENT LOYALTY AND REACTIVATING DORMANT CLIENTS

Strategy to secure client loyalty

Some companies are extremely successful in converting people into clients through aggressive commercial policies. Those same companies also manage to convert their clients into potential clients. They are, however, unaware of the necessity of securing client loyalty.

Acquiring a client costs five times the amount needed to secure loyalty. This means that when you lose a client, five times more resources will have to be applied to compensate for that loss. Such fruitless activities will lead a company to stagnation and eventually to regression. A consistent policy must be implemented to secure client loyalty for the company. The difficulty of adhering to such a policy increases with the number of clients a company has. It is obvious that a company like Publicis will have less difficulty in securing the loyalty of its 80 clients than a company like Renault, who has eight million clients. When Renault increases by one percentage point the number of repeat orders from clients, their yearly sales of 650,000 cars in the French market will be increased by 80,000 extra cars. This means any company should tackle the problem of securing client loyalty.

The approach will vary according to the type of product you are marketing. If you are selling equipment which your clients will buy over protracted cycles, for instance, once every two or three years, as is the case for cars, securing client loyalty is more difficult than in the case of shorter cycles. When purchases are made regularly at short intervals you must ensure regular, almost permanent contact with your customers. IBM, for example, employs a technical sales person totally dedicated to managing their Peugeot account.

Securing client loyalty may mean permanent contact if the client's importance requires it. Clients can be classified in five categories:

- occasional client
- frequent client
- regular client
- permanent client
- militant client.

The militant client is more than permanent; he/she is one whose attitude to your company is almost religious – for example, Apple computer fans.

Acquiring client loyalty means your policy must be to get your clients to move from being an occasional customer to the ideal situation where all your clients are militants who consider your product to be best in its field.

For example, car hire clients and the service industries (banking, insurance, etc.) and especially companies supplying business-to-business services will often attract militant clients.

In heavy industry products such as heavy vehicles or heavy load handling equipment are in a different situation. Such products are purchased over fairly long cycles, some years elapsing between two purchases. In industries such as computer equipment, for instance, the same company will be making short- and long-cycle sales.

The way one organises obtaining customer loyalty varies according to the size of the client. IBM has one technical sales person in its division servicing a single large client's account. In departments selling to small- and medium-sized companies, clients are more and more frequently handled by outside organisations, and the problem of securing loyalty is very different. The problem is particularly difficult in the case where clients are buying through third party wholesalers or dealers. Is the client who buys a Renault car from dealership X a client of Renault or of X? The same goes for the client who buys an IBM microcomputer from a retailer: whose client is he/she?

The problem must be looked at in terms of responsibility: from the moment Renault or IBM have a degree of responsibility to the client, that client is also theirs. In such cases the client is both a client of the brand and of the retailer. The manufacturer must adopt a policy to secure client loyalty which will adapt to the type of client, the distribution system, and the type of product that it is marketing.

Telemarketing will play its part in securing client loyalty every time it is not possible to ensure a permanent contact between a sales person and the client. Presence becomes the key word; Peugeot has clearly realised this as that is the code name of their whole programme for securing client loyalty.

The role of the telephone in securing client loyalty

Telemarketing will be effective in securing client loyalty when the sales person is unable to ensure a frequent and regular presence with a client. With the help of its immediate interactive possibilities and at a considerably cheaper cost than that of a visit, it is possible, with the help of telemarketing, to monitor clients to get proper feedback and to be in a position to send a sales person every time one is required. In particular, this may be used:

- to secure repeat sales
- to respond to a threat from competitors.

In this way your client feels important and does not feel, as often happens, that once a sale has been made the manufacturer has lost interest. Telemarketing will act in conjunction with mailings to maintain a determined cycle of repeat orders. The frequency of mailings and telephone calls will vary according to need, repeat purchase habit, and pressure coming from competitors.

A sales person for a well-known car dealers in America sends a postcard to each one of his clients at least once a month. He calls them on the phone at least twice a year and manages in this way to secure the loyalty of his existing clients. However, while this is an excellent example of a quality sales person it does not solve the problem of sales productivity.

The method selected by companies such as Peugeot, Rover and IBM is more efficient. These companies have automated, with the help of data processing facilities, their system for securing client loyalty so that it conforms to specified levels.

At a given time, a letter or telephone call-sheet is automatically produced from the client data base. Various letter formats and telephone scripts are used to ensure maximum effectiveness at each stage of the life cycle of the equipment purchased by the client. The number of contacts taking place over a three-year period can reach twenty, shared between mailings and telephone calls. Specialist phoners use the various scripts to ensure maximum efficiency. In terms of actual organisation, Rover has selected a decentralised system whereas Peugeot has set up a centralised system.

Each phoning cycle must be designed according to the ownership cycle of the vehicle. The body of data processed on the phone is supplied by data processing, so the system can manage hundreds of thousands of clients. Telephone calls are made at least once a year:

- Within the first month after a purchase in order to get feedback about client satisfaction.
- In the second year to mark the first anniversary of the car purchase.
- In the third year to mark the second anniversary and to obtain feedback concerning any buying intention. Thereafter, calls are made every six months to track such intentions.

For companies supplying services, the telephone can be used to secure client loyalty when the product is purchased more or less regularly, for example, in the car hire business or office supplies. Telemarketing can then help to develop sales by monitoring client satisfaction after each sale. This is cost-effective for clients such as car hire clients who have just spent over £1,000 on their last purchase. The client will feel acknowledged by this proof of care and will go on using the same supplier.

In the area of industrial consumables which are purchased for instance every four months, it is possible to have a programme to secure client loyalty by contacts on the phone every two months. Two different scripts can be used:

- a goodwill contact on the phone if there is no particular purchasing requirement
- a selling and promotional script if a requirement has been expressed or if no order has been obtained during the previous call.

The key to any policy aimed at securing client loyalty is to understand that any contact with clients, by whichever means, must not systematically be considered a selling action. This type of contact we call a goodwill contact. The decision by top management to initiate such a contact is the starting point of a true policy of securing client loyalty. A client must not be viewed at all times as a buyer and client care must be handled in versatile ways. Sales must be looked upon as a service to the client and not as the short-term successful placement of some equipment. The companies who will be ensured of success in the future are those who understand the real meaning of service. Acquiring client loyalty and using telemarketing are part of that understanding.

Reactivating clients

The first stage in any policy aimed at securing client loyalty is to reactivate your client list. If for years you have not engaged in any systematic communication and you then decide to set up a policy, you already have a history of interactions with each client and possibly some black marks. Reactivating old clients is therefore necessary to avoid losing them.

This is a mistake frequently made by companies who approach new clients with a new policy in that field while old clients who have practically turned into prospects are forgotten. These must be reactivated, and telemarketing is one of the basic tools used for doing this.

How should one contact clients who have received no news from you for some years? You have only two possibilities:

- Either you organise a goodwill call to communicate with these clients in the framework of a market survey; or
- You take the opportunity of a new product launch to call those clients and invite them to a demonstration.

In the latter case it is clear that the launch must be reserved for existing clients of the brand. Phone Marketing organised such a market share recovery for the launch of the Peugeot 405 car, which was extremely successful. All Peugeot buyers of the period 1977–80 were called on the phone to be invited to a pre-preview so they could examine the Peugeot 405 before anyone else. This worked extremely well. Twenty thousand out of 100,000 people contacted on the phone came to look at the new model in the course of a ten-day period before the official launch.

A survey carried out among these clients revealed that after this telemarketing campaign:

- 95 per cent of clients felt acknowledged by this invitation
- 75 per cent of clients intended to keep their loyalty to Peugeot
- 50 per cent of clients declared that they intended to buy a 405 in the course of that year
- 62 per cent of clients gave preference to the phone as against any other means of regular communication with the brand.

By making this contact with the owners of 305 and 505 models, Peugeot underlined that existing clients were not forgotten. This does not happen very often and should be highlighted.

It is difficult to know exactly how many clients will go on to buy a Peugeot as a consequence of the campaign for securing loyalty but the question that should really be asked is: 'If nothing is done to secure client loyalty are your chances any better than if you set up a proper policy with that aim?' No executive would dare say that would be the case. Reactivating client lists and securing client loyalty fits into the general trend of company management, and telemarketing is the most obvious support tool. There is no limit to telemarketing applications in this field; it is possible to contact clients dating back ten years.

Conditions for success

It is useful to examine the conditions needed to use telemarketing successfully in securing client loyalty.

Peugeot Motor America, an American subsidiary of Peugeot, sells 15,000 new cars each year and has 70,000 clients. In the past, because their dealer network was not coherent and because of mistakes made by the management, a number of Peugeot clients found they had problems with their vehicles. In 1987 Peugeot decided to initiate a policy of customer care which meant calling each Peugeot client at least once a year, which meant 70,000 calls a year.

Peugeot considers that one of their vehicle users must not be cut off from dialogue with the company for more than one year. As telemarketing is the only medium available to have a dialogue, apart from face-to-face contact with the sales people in the dealerships, a campaign was undertaken by Phone Marketing in the United States.

A team of eight phoners working half time over the whole year was set up in the New York offices to call every client. These were goodwill calls and not to make a sale. However, in 10 per cent of cases clients expressed a short-term intention to purchase and this was then communicated to the Peugeot dealer for the follow-up.

The objective, however, was to secure loyalty to Peugeot by acknowledging the client. Peugeot's objective was for medium-term results in this campaign which was a simple and effective operation.

The keys to the successful operation of Phone Marketing America were:

- determination on the part of top management that clients should be tracked
- a soft-approach script
- operations supervised by a professional in the car business
- continuity in the team of phoners.

The phoners who worked on this campaign were chosen for their good communication skills. They were not under pressure to close a sale but were aware of servicing the client. This involves adopting a completely different psychological approach.

Another campaign for securing client loyalty set up by a company is the Diac club of Renault agents. It is a method by which four times a year the 1,500 top agents in the Renault network are communicated with on behalf of the Renault financing arm, the Diac. Once every quarter the Diac club agents are called up on the phone and asked to answer questions which are part of a yearly competition. Each correct answer means the allocation of points which, when added up, allow the agent to win luxury trips. Even if the agent does not win, the fact that he or she is a member of the Diac club encourages loyalty to the network.

In this way Diac has set up, by means of the club, not only a means of securing loyalty, but also a real training method in the questionnaires, and a tool for motivation in the competition. Agents who used to complain that they were only acknowledged by the dealerships now feel closer to the Diac. The dealers can now feel that the agents have a good knowledge of financial products and Diac is in a position to develop sales with both dealers and agents.

This example of a more sophisticated approach shows that creativity in establishing a strategic global communication policy using telemarketing is a key element of success.

18

UNUSUAL USES
OF TELEMARKETING

Serving the consumer

On all Proctor product packages in the United States there is a freephone number through which you can access a telemarketing centre dedicated to Proctor, called Proctor Customer Service. About twenty phoners are employed by this service to answer client calls. After each call the client is sent a letter confirming the conversation or answering specific questions. This system receives 200,000 calls every year and ensures the consumer can get an answer to any problem or question concerning any of the products. Another important aspect of this service is the volume of feedback given to Proctor's marketing. In one instance, the packaging of a toothpaste was modified as a consequence of feedback obtained through this consumer service.

All the information collected is entered in a data processing system which then analyses market data. Each month a report is read from the consumer service at management meetings. This Proctor service illustrates a new method of using the telephone to service consumers.

In Europe companies such as Proctor, Colgate and Nestlé have organised consumer service departments on the telephone following the same model. Colgate offers a service using a team of in-house phoners working in conjunction with a data capture operation to produce marketing data. This means the consumer has permanent access to the manufacturer and the manufacturer's marketing services are supplied with on-going feedback.

Consumer service operations have also been organised in the car industry, in particular for customer care, and have in time developed towards being general information centres.

Citroën has a freephone number that can be called at any time.

At Peugeot or at Renault there is a service which, without a freephone number, is specialised in client help and can give information on all the maker's models. Citroën's service receives about 10,000 queries each month in addition to help calls. At IBM the same phone-in number appears on all communication or advertising documents.

Integrating the telephone

In some companies, different phone numbers appear on advertisements, on stationery, or in brochures. This produces a degree of confusion for people contacting the company. Some companies such as Bull or Club Med have made the effort to set up a telephone number which puts the caller through to a central service (called Bull-Info in the Bull company). This method is now being implemented in other companies with the objective of providing the company with a centre combining telephone and data processing operations.

Five years ago Bull noticed there was an important wastage of telephone calls and decided to set up a system that would deal efficiently with 'orphan' phone calls wandering from one department to the other. This became the Bull-Info service. The company invested in four areas:

- telephone and data processing equipment
- setting up a team of ten dedicated specialists
- training and organising the team
- internal communication campaign.

The success of such a system rests with the members of the communication service team. Half a million pounds was spent in data processing equipment and software. It is now possible for an operator to answer questions with the help of a single key word. If this is not enough, the operator can carry out investigations and call back with the answer. The question and the answer given are then entered in a data processing system which then builds up a database which is the living memory of the company.

The specialist phoners were selected from technical sales people and people who had over fifteen years' experience of the company. The team was trained over a period of two months before starting on the job. An internal communication campaign was then implemented so that the 20,000 Bull employees should be aware of and appreciate the value of the system and the behavioural adjustment in the company.

At least once a month a top executive of some large group visits Bull-Info to see the installations in Louveciennes. The company has truly succeeded in setting up a system to process consumer calls which is becoming a standard. More and more companies are implementing this type of service which needs the commitment of top management in view of its strategic aspects concerning communications.

Credit control

Companies supplying financial services in France, such as Cetelem or Cofica, have set up telephone operations to recover bad debts. In many cases the telephone script resembles the following:

- Mr Smith, you bought a Toyota car in 1984, didn't you?
- Yes, that is correct.
- Mr Smith, in your general behaviour do you consider you are honest or dishonest?
- I am honest.
- Right, Mr Smith, so why is it that you have not paid the three last instalments on that car? etc. . . .

This approach may appear aggressive, but attitudes and script in debt recovery are quite different from other uses of telemarketing. The phoner profiles must also be different, and they should be mature people. It is an activity which needs a really well-adjusted personality to recover overdue payments from, say, a divorced woman with two children who has to live on a small amount a month.

There are debt recovery operations which are not as delicate, in particular in the business-to-business field. An increasing number of small- and medium-sized companies in France do not pay their bills at the date they are due, forcing the supplier to wait. If the supplier stays passive the waiting may be protracted. The manager of a small- or medium-sized company is waiting for a phone call before she pays, on the principle that if the supplier does not call he is feeling no urgency to be paid. When a supplier has up to 50 clients an assistant book-keeper can do this credit control. When there are hundreds of clients it is necessary to set up a proper telemarketing structure which is not only capable of recovering overdues, but will anticipate payment dates. To call up a client's accounts department to remind them that the payment date is coming up in three days can even be considered a service. I can guarantee that a series of three phone calls judiciously made will reduce by 30 days at least the time taken by clients to pay you:

- first call one week before payment date
- second call one week after payment was due
- third call two weeks after payment was due.

After the third call 95 per cent of clients will have paid. Debt recovery from clients in a business-to-business environment is merely a matter of setting up and organising a credit control service. The approach, however, must be such that you are not creating commercial problems for yourself. The original call before the date of payment must be extremely friendly as the client is not in default. The script of such a phone call is obviously quite different from the script of a call made six months after payment was due. A professional approach in this type of action will not only improve cashflow but will also contribute to securing client loyalty.

Motivating distributors

When any important information has to be communicated to the company's distribution network, such as the launch of a new advertising campaign or a new range of products, the nomination of a new Chief Executive or sending New Year greetings, it is important to discover new ways of getting the message across. It is always possible to organise a convention and to have a meeting of 600 distributors, or a video can be sent to each distributor through the field sales representatives' network. However, telemarketing offers an original and inexpensive method: the telemessage. A 60 second message appropriate to the event can be recorded by one of the company's top people. For instance, the sales director can be announcing the details of a new advertising campaign or the Chair can send season's greetings to all the managers. This one-minute message recorded in a studio, each expression, word and tone having been well worked out, can be used both on out-going and in-coming calls.

On out-going calls the 600 distributors or the managers can be called within a period of two days; the phoner starts the call and then runs the pre-recorded message. On in-coming calls it is possible to send a mailing with the phone number to be called to each of the targeted people and, when they call, the message can be delivered either automatically or after contact is made with a phoner.

PART III

OUTSTANDING TELEMARKETING CASE HISTORIES

MÉMOREX

The catalogue

The Mémorex catalogue has met with considerable success in France over a period of four years. To a great extent this is the result of an appropriate use of the telephone in conjunction with a catalogue, a strategy which was adopted right from the start. Mémorex has now decided to extend the method applied in France to all the other main European countries. The company naturally used the telephone in all its subsidiaries.

Joseph de la Taille, the International Director of Mémorex, and Jean-Luc Redoux, Director for France, and Alain Charpentier made these comments.

- *How was the Mémorex catalogue initiated?*
  Joseph de la Taille: Mémorex sells and maintains data processing peripherals for IBM computers as well as magnetic media consumables. We are also a European multinational. Four years ago, we launched in France a mail-order catalogue. It contains between 1,000 and 1,200 references exclusively on consumables and data processing accessories, such as screen stands, printer stands, or light furniture. This catalogue is published twice a year in 300,000 copies. What Mémorex has done which is special is to set up an integrated phoning service which works seamlessly with the catalogue. This service makes 40,000 client contacts each year.

- *Why was this catalogue created?*
  Jean-Luc Redoux: So as to process a considerable volume of small orders, each of which was worth on average £200; the catalogue is an ideal means to sell light equipment and to be close enough to the consumer to be able to serve him quickly.

- *What about the telemarketing unit?*
  Jean-Luc Redoux: We set it up so as to increase the catalogue's performance. Demand has to be stimulated continuously so as to increase turnover and increase the number of catalogue users. If you make the effort of calling your clients, for instance, to ask them if they have received your catalogue or to draw their attention to a promotional campaign, it is possible to sell more and faster. This confirms what we have already said: the telephone makes it possible to process a lot of small clients and to save the cost of visits. Additionally, the telephone makes it possible to run one-off promotional campaigns. Lastly, a very important aspect: updating client information.

- *What are your projects for Europe?*
  Alain Charpentier: Following on the success we have met with in France, we are going to develop the same integrated telemarketing system in West Germany, Italy, the UK and Benelux. And here I wish to mention that this is the first time an international campaign will be set up based on a French experiment. We are starting in Italy this month. In November we will start in Germany and then in the other countries.

- *What other lesson can you draw from this experience?*
  Alain Charpentier: Success needs perfect cooperation between the catalogue operation and the company running the telephone marketing campaign.

ATLAS COPCO

Telemarketing to support distributors

Atlas Copco uses a service company to run prospecting campaigns on the phone with the aim of gathering information to support distributors' sales operations. This has proved to be an effective method of establishing close links between the manufacturer and the distributors, and of creating sales.

Christian Laporte, Director of Atlas Copco, and Joël de Lanlay, Head of Marketing comment:

- *What are the main characteristics of Atlas Copco France?*
  Joël de Lanlay: It is one of the 46 sales companies – fourth in size according to its turnover – belonging to the Swedish multinational Atlas Copco, which has specialised in compressed-air equipment for industry, mining and quarry works, for building and public works. The French company sells the whole range of products, its yearly sales run at £45 million, it has 430 employees and runs ten agencies. The sales network employs 70 sales people and 200 distributors.

- *What is the role of distributors in the market?*
  Joël de Lanlay: We consider the global market to be about £200 million, 35 per cent of which is in building and public work and 65 per cent in industry. There are about 100,000 potential clients of whom 30,000 to 35,000 are in the first sector of industry, the rest being in secondary and tertiary industries, such as garages, transport, etc. Our market is therefore extremely fragmented and distributors are important for our penetration with small- and medium-sized companies. Our aim is to develop their turnover while avoiding situations where our sales people and theirs prospect the same client.

- *How did you eventually decide to use the telephone?*
  Christian Laporte: We were facing two problems: the cost of communication media addressing a fragmented market where unitary purchases were low, and the need to have an effect on the sales operations of distributors as these always tend to imitate the manufacturer.

- *What was the effect of your first campaign?*
  Christian Laporte: The first discussions we had with Phone Marketing were in May 1981. In October we carried out some tests. Results of these tests were analysed and full-scale operations started in February 1982.
  Joël de Lanlay: Using a list covering the Paris area, in which we make the greatest number of sales, we selected 18,000 leads. We screened them with the help of Phone Marketing and ended up with 12,000 company telephone numbers. These companies were called and it was possible to determine who was the person in charge of compressed-air equipment, and to detect their needs. Out of the 12,000, 6,000 which showed potential were qualified. We obtained in this way a basic prospecting list on which to concentrate the efforts of the sales force.
  Christian Laporte: The information collected by Phone Marketing was sorted according to the objectives we had defined and then communicated to distributors.

- *How did the distributors react?*
  Christian Laporte: During the test two out of four distributors and their sales force had expressed their satisfaction and two others had reservations because they feared we would be controlling their activities. Today we see that distributors feel extremely favourable because they feel that the prospecting we undertake really promotes their sales significantly and creates close links between the manufacturer and the distributors. For the last two years we have been repeating this operation three to four times a year with satisfactory results.

- *What are the actual results of those two years?*
  Christian Laporte: We have analysed the level of sales obtained on the selected market. Our starting base of 100 sales progressed to 120 in the areas where Phone Marketing had not been operating and to 290 in the areas where Phone

Marketing were operating. This is sufficient proof of the effectiveness of phoning in our industry.

- *What actions are you taking with your own sales people?*
  Christian Laporte: We also run telephone operations for our own sales force concerning products with much higher unitary values than those sold by distributors – seven or eight times as much – and addressing 1,200 companies in the Paris area. The fact that our sales people ask for prospecting and prospect-qualifying campaigns on the phone shows that in our operations these methods have matured and are now accepted as a matter of course. We also run this type of campaign through Phone Marketing who have extensive knowledge of industrial businesses.

BULL

Successful integration of phoning and data processing

For all companies, any information request which is not satisfied will detract from the company's image and may lose them sales. A recent study showed that large French companies lose 5 to 10 per cent of their sales as a result of poor handling of in-coming calls. As a consequence of having understood this clearly, Bull developed with Phone Marketing a particularly sophisticated information service, applying both the telephone and data processing within the framework of a communications technology system orientated not only externally but also internally. Here are the comments of two managers in the Bull organisation, Jacques Gauthier and Catherine Enck.

- *What are the key figures of the Bull group?*
  Catherine Enck: In 1984, turnover was £1,600 million showing an increase of 18.6 per cent on the previous year. Of those sales, 36.6 per cent were made abroad. This placed Bull in the lead European position, immediately behind IBM. The number of employees is 26,600.

- *How did the collaboration between Bull and Phone Marketing start?*
  Jacques Gauthier: With the help of a telephone survey we found that 32 per cent of information requests, ie. about 20,000 per year, were not being satisfied. As a result of this the group's general management decided to address the problem and to set up a system under the auspices of the 'Direction de l'Information et de la Communication' (Information and Communication Management). This system was then called 'Centre d'Information Bull'.

- *Was an answer found to the problem of 'wasted calls'?*
  Jacques Gauthier: The service set up under the name of Bull Info now employs five people with business and engineering training who identify the problems, search for the correct person among the Bull personnel to give an answer, and establish the connection. To set up operations, it was arranged that they meet all the units in the group before this service was launched so that they should be well-known and so that they should know who to go to; they were then given a Phone Marketing training in telephone skills; they then did some voice work with radio announcers.

  During the same period and following Phone Marketing's recommendations, we created awareness of the system and its aims among all our personnel.

- *How was this achieved?*
  We first created a work group with trainers, teachers, and psychologists with whose help practical solutions were defined: Features were inserted in our internal newsletter concerning the telephone and the Bull Info service, basic rules on telephone management were established, and every member of the company received a plastic memo card outlining the appropriate use of the telephone and the internal equipment, etc. At the same time, telephone operators were trained in better professional skills.

- *Which tools were installed for the 'Centre d'Information Bull'?*
  Jacques Gauthier: With the help of the G.CAM, we built a database – 'Banque d'Information Bull' (BIB) which contains answers to all questions on the structures, entities and people who are in a position to supply information. We also set up a second database of questions in which are recorded all calls received and processed by the 'Centre d'Information Bull'. The Bull Info personnel use these two databases. Information in the BIB will gradually be available to all members of personnel through a network of video text-type terminals. It will eventually be possible to access these from external events sites.

- *What lessons can you draw from this system?*
  Jacques Gauthier: What is striking in this set-up is that the telephone and data processing are now working together. They will have created a real computerised communication tool.

CRÉDIT AGRICOLE

The bank card event

In August 1984 the Carte Bleu group (a French visa card) the Caisse Nationale Du Crédit Agricole and the Crédit Mutuel (large popular French banks) signed an agreement creating the bank card. The first network distributing this new card was the Crédit Agricole who promoted it through a system based on a multi-media communication strategy and a direct selling strategy using mailings and telemarketing. Jacques Lenormand, a Director of the Crédit Agricole, comments:

- *How important is the launching of the bank card for the Crédit Agricole?*
  Six million of our eleven million clients have a Crédit Agricole card. It is given free and has a rather limited function. Our challenge is to convert these cards into bank cards which have to be paid for. Our aim is to have issued four million cards by the end of 1985.

- *What are the means you applied to that end?*
  Knowing we could not consider getting four million clients to visit our agencies and be interviewed, we developed on the one hand a multi-media communication strategy (television, posters, radio, etc.) and on the other hand a strategy of direct sales using mailing in conjunction with the telephone.

- *What were the goals given to Phone Marketing?*
  The sights were set quite high: selling the card by telephone was to be tested and our network was then to be trained into selling the card based on proven performance.

- *What were the characteristics of the approaches made on the phone?*
  A bank does not sell products as such, but a banking relation. One of Crédit Agricole's trump cards is the quality of its

friendly relations with its clients. This had to be taken into account. Maintaining and using that relationship in a telephone script was a real challenge that was successfully tackled by Phone Marketing.

- *What were the results obtained during the test action?*
  The first tests showed that the fact that the card had to be paid for was not a problem. The main problems we met at times were to overcome considerations about using the card, or the absence of a real need for such a card.

- *After those tests, how was the strategy developed?*
  We are now setting up, with Phone Marketing, decentralised autonomous networks capable of applying direct marketing methods.

SOCIÉTÉ DES BAINS DE MER (SBM)

A strategy for business tourists

The Grand Prix, the casinos, the sunshine all make up Monte Carlo's traditional image. There are few companies in France who are aware of all the possibilities offered by the Société des Bains de Mer in the realm of business tourism. To create that awareness the SBM has set up a strategy of direct communication with the aim of detecting, informing and acquiring the loyalty of companies. Jean Morieux, Sales Director for SBM in France comments:

- *What are the economic facts about the SBM?*
  It is among the top 500 French companies listed on the stock exchange and is controlled by the government of Monaco. It employs about 2,200 people, half of whom work in the hotel business which accounts for one third of turnover, and the other half works in the casino activities which account for two thirds of the turnover.

- *How would you describe your company's activities?*
  Monte Carlo is a privileged site. The SBM can be described as a communication tool with a humanistic approach serving companies and in particular their needs in the area of business tourism. This is done with an approach aiming at high quality both in personnel and investments. Our objectives are to develop that position particularly with French companies.

- *What are the special features of SBM?*
  One aspect that French companies are not sufficiently aware of is that SBM, in addition to its hotel businesses which are currently still being perfected, can offer them the possibility of solving in every way all their problems relating to events

such as seminars, conferences, etc., while dealing with only one supplier. We also supply consultancy services which mean, thanks to infrastructures and policies promoted by the government of Monte Carlo in the area of entertainment, that it is possible to spend a whole week in Monaco without having to do anything twice.

- *By what means do you create awareness of all that is available?*
We started our sales communication strategy ten years ago. At that time, we set up our sales teams in Paris and then in New York and London and started using mailings, telex shots and the telephone. We now want to reach further and structure our efforts within the framework of an overall direct marketing strategy.

- *What is the part played by the telephone?*
In September 1984 we ran an initial test operation directed at 1,500 companies in the Paris area to identify who were the decision-makers for business tourism and to find out what their short- and medium-term plans might be. This allowed us to identify 225 previously unknown prospects who were given our message. In April 1985, a second (call-back) campaign was conducted to make appointments with the most promising companies; we are selective as the SBM offers upmarket products.

- *How is your identification and information policy implemented?*
At this moment we are launching a campaign to qualify, identify and contact companies with the help of new lists containing about 2,000 companies. Our aim is to determine, through successive screenings, the 500 companies who are the main users and who fit the criteria of quality and volume of movements which fit the facilities offered by Monte Carlo. We must naturally go beyond the stage of finding out who those companies are. After having made a strategic analysis we intend to recruit those 500 companies into a special club that will operate along specific programmes.

- *What have the first operations produced?*
Our objectives are for long-term relationships. Phoning operations have already enhanced the positive image of Monte Carlo and confirmed the fact that our message was well received. SBM has now developed a systematic method which is rationalised and uniquely ours by which we can be present at all large conventions, seminars, etc.

CITROËN

A second generation approach to using the telephone

At Citroën the telephone has long been integrated within sales operations and is part of internal trainings. This made it difficult to set up a new telephone strategy within the framework of a new customer care policy. Francis Roux, Head of Marketing at Citroën, makes useful comments:

- *How was a telephone approach fitted into your operations?*
  The 'Produits Méthodes Reseaux' department, created three years ago and with the emphasis on 'Méthodes', was looking for new means of following up clients within the framework of a new global commercial approach. We had noticed that our level of client loyalty was stagnant and that we had to do something to increase our chances of being present on an ongoing basis with our clients.

  We had realised the very powerful potential our existing clients represented. At the same time we also realised that the sales people within our dealers' operations – 1,600 sales people in France – were totally opposed to traditional methods of prospecting.

  We then decided to secure our on-going presence along commercial lines but not necessarily in an aggressive way. This was the origin of a meticulously defined strategy of repeated contacts based on the periodicity of repeat purchases. Four years represent the average but we have chosen to develop this strategy over the first two years using two main supports – mailings and phoning – as these fit harmoniously with the aims of such a policy. The methods offered by Phone Marketing confirmed our views.

- *How was that contact policy then implemented?*
  During the first two years after the purchase of a vehicle, the buyer is contacted through mailings sent by the dealership as a support to that purchase and to offer various services. These mailings are sent one month, eleven months, and finally 23 months after the purchase. After that two-year period, phoning, which is a fantastic tool for the sales rep to re-establish contact, will start.

- *What are the special features of this method?*
  In May 1984, during a first stage of operations, we met the eleven Citroën trainers to outline our strategy. We then gave them a manual with a cassette illustrating examples of using the script. These trainers were then trained themselves in writing telephone scripts and making phone calls. The trainers then started operations at the level of dealerships and subsidiaries, working in meetings with the sales people who then received remote training.

- *How was this remote training carried out?*
  One-hour training sessions were organised with simulated telephone conversations on progressively more sophisticated levels; the part of the client was played by the trainer. The sales rep's responses were recorded and after each conversation the trainer gave some feedback. After three months the original group of 956 sales people had been trained and we then asked dealers to install, as a follow-up, an on-going implementation of the method. The on-going follow-up is essential as the method must not be applied as a one-off. As positive results were obtained, a second set of trainings will be arranged for the sales people who have not been part of the first operation.

- *What conclusions can be drawn from this first collaboration?*
  The telephone is now definitely part of Citroën's culture. This is so true that we have recently used the telephone to get an important message through to our 400 dealerships over a period of two hours. The telephone will be successfully implemented within the framework of our new sales approach because the network is aware of a need. I believe no company in the car industry has gone as far as Citroën in the use of the telephone. Having acquired acceptance in the network, we now have a very powerful tool.

NIXDORF

A perfect example of integrated phoning

Nixdorf, a particularly dynamic company in a highly competitive market, has chosen to target the needs for turnkey computer applications. To enhance the effectiveness of its 150 technical sales people the department of general data processing chose to set up an integrated prospecting system with the phone. Here are some comments from Guy Jayat, Sales Director of the general data processing division.

- *How important is, and what is the scope of, the activity of the 'Division Informatique Générale' (General data processing division) of NIXDORF?*
  Of the company's turnover, 80 per cent of the £80 million obtained in 1984 came from two main divisions: banking and insurance, and general data processing. In the latter case, the market they are targeting is small- and medium-sized companies, retailers, local authorities, administrations, professional people, etc. We sell turnkey systems, which means we offer global solutions – integrating equipment, software, and personnel training.

- *What made you choose the telephone?*
  Over a few years our market has really become a consumer's market; a very wide market. We soon realised that 60 per cent of the working time of our sales force was spent searching for clients. This task could easily be taken on by other specialised personnel. This meant giving back to our technical sales people the time they needed for actual selling. It is pure logic for us increasingly to use direct marketing approaches and particularly telephone marketing.

142

- *What benefits do you see in this integration?*
  One of the important aspects of phoning is of course the detection of hot prospects, but it is also important to track warm and cold prospects. It is therefore important to implement a system of follow-up supported by a computerised database. In view of our type of activity it was easy for us to set up and manage such a system.

  It is that concept of 'system' which is most important. If a phoning operation is to produce maximum effectiveness it is essential to track further than hot prospects. The system is not exclusively a sales system but a method of being present in any transaction taking place in our markets.

- *How did things develop in the course of this integration?*
  We started off by carrying out tests among soft drink vendors. The tests gave positive results with a 20 per cent acceptance rate for appointments. We then selected a person among our personnel to supervise the service. Scripts were set up in collaboration, lists of prospects were compiled, etc. In fact, we set up a small in-house telemarketing team for which we recruited phoners with an appropriate sales profile who were then also trained. This team of five people plus the supervisor was then put to work. We are following operations with monthly in-house training at Nixdorf. This on-going importing of external skills is proving extremely effective.

CANON

Training the sales force

Canon gives special telephone skills training to their facsimile network field sales people. The aim is to up-date the prospects file and to increase sales. This has given spectacular results and a considerable increase in the amount of sales. Managers and field sales people dealing with facsimile equipment are unconditional advocates of the telephone, as François Stalin from Canon comments.

- *How is the Canon facsimile network structured?*
  In 1984 Canon wanted to set up a network of large distributors comprising small- and medium-sized independent companies employing 30 to 50 people but who would be selling exclusively Canon products. These were grouped under the title 'facsimile' to distinguish them from other multi-vendor sales outlets. If a comparison is to be made with the car industry, they are the Canon dealerships. Each facsimile distributor makes sales of between £100,000 and £150,000 per month. It is within the framework of this network that Canon decided to test the effectiveness of telephone marketing.

- *What was the brief given to Phone Marketing?*
  The facsimile managers and their sales people had to be made aware that the telephone is an extremely powerful prospecting and selling tool. In the first stage, training was given to the sales people, at our own premises, in appointment-setting on the phone. We then sent a team of phoners to the dealerships with the following goals: to identify and qualify prospects on the basis of a list supplied to the facsimiles network by Canon and to communicate leads to the sales team for making appointments.

- *Why did you start off giving training to the sales people before sending phoners to the facsimiles dealers?*
  This was specifically to create awareness of the telephone among sales people and to have them involved in this new method. The work done later by the phoners was better appreciated by them as they had practised it themselves and could understand its usefulness.

- *How many facsimile companies were involved in this training?*
  Nine up until now but within a few months each of our fourteen distributors will have been visited by Phone Marketing.

- *At this half-way point, what can be said about the results?*
  The telephone made it possible to identify 8 to 10 per cent of warm prospects in the lists processed by Phone Marketing. These actions certainly increased sales for the facsimile distributors. They also made it possible to build an up-to-date database for on-going use. Canon France use the database management system with every facsimile distributor. We are now in a position to run much more tightly targeted prospecting actions. We are now considering what action we can initiate to keep these databases active.

GOODYEAR

The telephone fills the field sales team's address book

Goodyear's heavy vehicles department recently set up telephone operations to support the sales team in the selection of 'good' prospects and making appointments. As a result, more than 10,000 useful contacts were made and considerable time was saved as the awareness of market conditions was spectacularly updated. Jean-Paul Cavelier, who is in charge of the heavy vehicles department at Goodyear, comments.

- *Can you give us some details on the heavy vehicles department of Goodyear?*
  This department was set up at the beginning of the 1980s with the objective to sell tyres to two main types of users: transport companies and industrial companies owning fleets of lorries. Goodyear's heavy vehicle department now has a 12 per cent market share in refitments; 5,000 fleets use our tyres. The main problem is that this market is highly fragmented – there are 50,000 transport companies in France, 75 per cent of which have less than five vehicles. The same situation exists with industrial fleets. The telephone is a necessary tool for prospecting such a fragmented market.

- *What suggested the use of telephone marketing?*
  We needed something to support the actions of our sales people who carry an enormous workload. They must prospect, sell, ensure the follow-up, and give us feedback on the developments of requirements in the market, so that we can design future products. The telephone makes it possible rapidly to detect the good prospects, especially in areas where we are not particularly well-established.

146

- *What is the set-up of your telephone action?*
  We selected the best list, of 'transport companies and industrial companies owning more than fifteen trucks'. We then contacted these prospects on the phone so as to qualify them in two respects: first, to obtain acceptance of a contact; second, to collect as much information as possible to support the field sales rep's visit. Every Saturday, each field sales rep receives at home the list of contacts that have been set up in his/her area. It is then possible for each rep to organise their work for the next week as from Monday morning.

- *How did you go about involving the sales force?*
  I visited the management of every area. We explained to the sales people what our purpose was. We showed them the scripts for the phone calls.

- *How did the sales people react?*
  They all backed us. This kind of support cannot be refused! Our actions supplied them with opportunities they were absolutely unaware of. Particularly when overworked, a sales rep will tend always to work the same clients. The telephone allowed them to widen their operation. Their telephone skills were also improved, though we did not give them any particular training in that area.

- *What were the overall results?*
  The campaign is not over, but within a year we will have covered the whole territory and more than 10,000 qualified contacts will have been made. This operation is giving us an excellent knowledge of the market and we are now in a position to quantify with great accuracy the required number of sales people in each area. Also, the telephone has not only been a means to acquire new clients, but we find that existing clients are quite pleased to see that we are taking an interest in them!

FORD AGRICOLE

Agricultural products' dealers are involved in the manufacturer's prospecting action

Whereas Ford is the second largest supplier of agricultural tractors in the world, in France the company only stands in sixth place, but has decided to remedy this at short notice. The strategy they selected was to be present whenever a possible purchase in their field was being considered. The telephone was considered an effective and selective prospecting tool for the support of the dealerships. Jacques Richard from Ford Agricole comments.

- *What is the position of Ford France?*
  Ford France is only the sixth largest supplier of agricultural machines in France; Renault is number one and Fiat number two. This position does not reflect our overall position in the world, where we are number two, nor in many other European markets. In the 1960s and 1970s, Ford supplied between 8 and 10 per cent of the market in number of units. But mainly because our products were becoming obsolete, our deliveries had dropped to 4.9 per cent in 1981.

- *What was your strategy to remedy this?*
  By the end of 1981 we launched a new range of products that fitted the market's requirements. At the same time we set up a strategy of goals aiming to recapture the lost ground. Over the last three years our real growth has been 5.5 per cent in 1982, 6.4 per cent in 1983 and 7.7 per cent at the end of July last year. When we started out on this recapture, we assumed that market share is a function of two ratios: the percentage of purchase opportunities at which you are present, and the per cent conversion of these opportunities. Having the best

product, the best prices, the best marketing only has an effect on the second ratio and is useless if you are not present at every opportunity.

- *How can that be achieved?*
We increased the number of our dealerships. They are now 140 and we are aiming at between 160 and 180. Also, by ensuring that their sales force is present at a maximum number of opportunities. This presence is expensive for our dealerships. Some have reduced their structures and because of that situation we have designed a methodology to regain market share through prospecting actions.

- *How did Ford's collaboration with the telephone develop?*
In July 1983 a telemessage campaign was targeted to the dealers so as to give the dealership management an awareness of telephone techniques. Towards the end of 1983, we ran a test operation in the Cavaillon area involving 5,000 leads in agricultural enterprises. This test was extremely enlightening. We found out that we had underestimated by a wide margin the rate of positive response – 30 per cent of people contacted agreed to make an appointment – and our dealers' sales force was overwhelmed with the number of opportunities they had to follow up.

- *What lesson is to be drawn from this experiment?*
We analysed the results obtained and then arranged to set up with our dealerships towards the beginning of 1984 operations for which we undertook to pay half the cost.

  Thirty-five of our main dealerships expressed an interest. We described to them the results of the test made in Cavaillon, and during May and June we launched with a number of them a prospecting campaign targeting 10,000 leads. We are now starting a new campaign targeting 25,000 leads with another group of dealers.

- *What was the dealers' reaction to these campaigns?*
Many consider that just the up-dating of their prospect list was worth the cost. They also realised that sales opportunities develop over a period of time.

- *How is this policy going to develop in the future?*
The next step is to integrate this activity within the dealerships. Now that they are familiar with the method they

realise that such campaigns can be run on a regular basis in-house. Another advantage of operating in-house is that it is possible to set up new actions at short notice. This requirement is possibly more important in our area of activity than in others because the field sales reps in a dealership do not only sell tractors but dozens of other products. Such operations help them to have more time available for selling tractors.

KODAK

Tactical and strategic phoning operations

Telemarketing made an unobtrusive entrance at Kodak France some three years ago. Little by little awareness spread to all departments. At this point Kodak France is setting up an in-house telemarketing structure. This shows that in addition to obtaining punctual tactical results telemarketing can modify global attitudes. Roger Glicksman, a member of Kodak's management team, comments.

- *How did Kodak France come to use telemarketing?*
  About four years ago, after having become aware of Kodak's telemarketing operations in the United States, the French management decided to investigate opportunities in France. A market survey followed. A meeting with Phone Marketing convinced me that such techniques, if used systematically, could increase the company's effectiveness.

- *What was the first actual implementation?*
  We immediately realised the support that could be obtained from telemarketing as an inexpensive prospecting tool. Three years ago we launched a campaign for our graphic arts products aimed at detecting and qualifying prospects. This was extremely successful. I must, however, mention that we first had to gain acceptance from the sales force for the idea that the telephone could be useful. Sales in that department have considerably increased. Telemarketing has certainly played a major role.

- *How were these experiments followed up?*
  By involving another department: the department of office equipment, and particularly the section dealing with microfilm. For this product we launched a campaign to invite

prospects to come to special events in our premises. The campaign was a call-back on a mailing invitation. The rate of response was in the order of 28 per cent.

- *And after the screening of prospects and ensuring the success of an event, what other applications did you implement?*
  In a third type of operation we found that telemarketing could, in certain specific cases, be more informative than a traditional type of market survey. For instance, in the case of specialised equipment, it was possible by phone to identify warm and hot prospects, to invite them to a meeting and determine the precise target profile for those products.

  We carried on with our survey. For instance, in our photocopier division the information we gathered allowed us to manage our field sales people's visits better. We then started training our sales force. In the same way, account managers in our Southern Distribution Centres are trained in taking orders and repeat purchase orders on the phone.

- *What is to be learned from all these experiments?*
  We now observe that all departments are implementing telemarketing operations in their sales structure. The same trend is taking place in the area of training. There certainly has been a change in outlook within Kodak France. The efforts we have made to create awareness have shown that the telephone is a productivity tool. There is now a next step.

- *What is to be that next step?*
  We asked ourselves: 'What if we did our own telemarketing?' On one hand, we knew that we couldn't have as sophisticated an operation as the one run by Phone Marketing. On the other hand a specialised team could run a number of simple out-going and in-coming operations and work as a link between the company and its clients in a most effective way. At the same time, with the experience gained from the external organisation, the team's professional skills could be developed. This unit serving all divisions will play a very important part. It will also be a way to test out all new means of telecommunications.

- *How is this new set-up going to be announced?*
  We are at present preparing audio-visual aids for all Kodak France personnel. This proves that telemarketing concerns everybody and also that the top management now considers it a fully-fledged communication tool, internally and externally.

VEDETTE

Acquiring market share

How can a brand selling to 3 per cent of the market increase its market share when the target population consists of professional buyers? This is the challenge Vedette had to meet for its range of 'Built in' products. The challenge was met with the help of a mix of communication techniques among which telemarketing played a key role. This is how it happened. Pierre Favre, Head of Sales at Vedette, explains.

- *Within the Vedette brand what is the position of the 'Built in' range?*
  Vedette, which is a brand name of Surmelec which is one of Thomson's five subsidiaries, enjoys a remarkable track record in the field of domestic electrical appliances. This is due to the quality of products, to the quality of staff and of course to the publicity given by 'Mère Denis'. (Mère Denis has become a well-known French television personality promoting Thomson appliances.) Mère Denis has an image which makes it easy for her to sell any washing machine, possibly also dishwashers and cookers, but is not well positioned for selling refrigerators and complete kitchen furniture with top market integrated units such as those Vedette launched four years ago. Our objective for those products is to distance ourselves from the classical image given by Mère Denis.

- *What is Vedette integrated furniture's position in its targeted market?*
  Sales development has been slow but regular since the launch which means that market share is now a little more than 3 per cent in volume. In the area of distribution, we have intentionally targeted specialist kitchen fitters while avoiding the 'easy' distribution channels. The choice was made because of the image we wanted to maintain and because the majority of sales are made through that channel.

- *Why did you resort to the telephone?*

We wished not only to motivate our sales force but also to create market awareness of the Vedette brand of integrated furniture among professional kitchen fitters. This we decided to do through a global prospecting campaign. We traditionally communicated with our targets through regular mailings sent every four months using Jacques Mandorla's company, Futurs Direct.

- *How was this new action implemented?*

Well, as I said, our target was professional kitchen fitters as well as a few department stores who had a specific department for kitchens, and some wholesalers: a total of 1,600 to 1,800 people. The first thing we did was to buy a list from a company specialised in the training of kitchen fitters. We decided to use the telemessage technique developed by Phone Marketing with a message recorded by myself, during which I outlined the characteristics of the range, Vedette's policies and the newly launched product. During the call the phoner then suggested an appointment with a consultant. At the same time the phoner qualified the target by asking what product she was used to installing, and the volume of installations she had previously made.

- *This campaign was just a telemessage then?*

No. Before the telemarketing campaign, we had sent out a mailing describing the product and an advertising campaign in the professional magazines was launched at the same time as the phoning. A seminar had also been organised for the sales people dealing with integrated furniture and other products in all areas of our market. The aim was to involve them in the whole operation and to inform them about kitchen fitters and their needs.

- *What results were obtained from this operation?*

The appointment setting rate was 55 per cent. The exact figure was 841 kitchen fitters who agreed to an interview with our field sales people. At this stage the operation has certainly created considerable awareness among kitchen fitters of the Vedette brand name in this specialised market of integrated kitchen furniture.

EUROPCAR

Identifying new car hire clients

In a service industry as highly competitive as the car hire business it is vital to actively seek out new clients. Europcar uses the phone to select new target companies. The objective is to direct the sales force towards hot prospects and to establish a dialogue with all the others. Guy Dauchez, Marketing Director at Europcar comments.

- *What is Europcar's position in the French market?*
  Three large companies dominate the market. We are the leader in the business-to-business segment and have a 30 per cent share of that market. Europcar is present nationally through 260 offices, of which 210 are franchised.

- *What are the developments in that market?*
  A very strong expansion took place after 1970. The first slow-down appeared at the beginning of 1984 as a result of the change in the VAT rate from 18.6 to 33.33 per cent and because of budget cuts in many companies. Since last October, however, there is a renewal of activity.

- *How did things go for Europcar?*
  In spite of the slow-down we had a reasonably good year and our rate of growth was greater than the average growth of the market, but 1984 was quite a difficult year during which we had to learn tight targeting and increased management efficiency.

- *What made you decide to use telemarketing?*
  We have a fairly classic type of sales force. We wished to find a way of increasing their performance, particularly in terms of prospecting activities for gaining new markets and new clients. We wished to direct our sales force towards specified

155

targets. We felt small- and medium-sized companies were a valuable target, but to verify this it was necessary to establish contact. This was not possible using traditional means and for this it was necessary to have recourse to the telephone.

- *How was the screening implemented?*
  During June of this year a campaign screened 2,500 companies in Paris and the Paris area. The script had been carefully designed and detected existing needs and collected information on regular needs. After analysing the opportunities that were uncovered, Europcar was in a position to direct the sales team towards the hottest prospects to close an immediate contract. Also, where needs were less important, a direct communications strategy was followed with a view to provoking automatic response through the offer of a new service in the form of a membership card and a mailings scenario to ensure on-going relationships.

- *What were the results of this prospecting?*
  In the first stage the appointment-setting rate was more than 10 per cent with the most valuable prospects. The results have to be assessed over a period of time before full results can be evaluated.

- *Following this experiment, what is Europcar going to be doing?*
  This screening operation has been cost-effective in actual results with respect to database building, contacts, new contracts, etc. We have decided to pursue our campaigning towards small- and medium-sized companies. The aim is to find out exactly how support can be provided for the sales force. We are also examining what actions can be taken to ensure client loyalty as this is a vital aspect of the services industry and the telephone is certainly one of the most effective tools to that end.

AIR INTER

Sales grow wings

Air passenger transport must consider two-figure growth as a thing of the past. Air Inter has decided to use telemarketing in the search for new markets in the business-to-business segment. Gilbert Petit de Mirbeck and Gérard Jouron of Air Inter comment.

- *What are the significant figures concerning Air Inter?*
  Gérard Jouron: Air Inter is number one in the internal flights market serving 28 cities every day. Ten and a half million passengers are carried every year, ie. about 30,000 every day. This represents 2,225,000 clients among whom 60 per cent are travelling for professional reasons and 40 per cent for private reasons.

- *What is the structure of your sales organisation?*
  Gilbert Petit de Mirbeck: There is a sales management for Paris and the Paris region in the wider sense, and four provincial managements located in Marseilles, Lyon, Toulouse and Strasbourg. The Paris area accounts for 44 per cent of turnover and 42 per cent of the traffic volume.

- *How are your clients processed commercially?*
  Gérard Jouron: Clients travelling for personal reasons are wooed through the media in general. Companies and travel agents are visited by our sales people. In Paris and the Paris area, we have about 8000 client companies and relations are processed by a computer system called Seric – Système d'Enrigistrement Rationnel des Informations Commerciales (Rational Recording System of Sales Information).

- *Why use the telephone?*
  Gérard Jouron: In our business-to-business relations we wish

to find new business methods which allow contact with tight markets where the unitary size of sales does not justify the full intervention of our sales team (54 people covering the whole of France), when cost and time factors are taken into account.

Gilbert Petit de Mirbeck: This led us to set up a test in the Paris area to examine the possibility of setting up more effective methods than those implemented in the past.

- *What were the objectives of this experiment?*

Gérard Jouron: The aim was to determine the travel potential of targeted companies, so that sales operations could be better managed. Telemarketing collected information concerning the need or absence of need for making visits at a distance of more than 400 kilometres. This campaign also recorded the names and job positions of the people in charge of travelling. There was also a prospecting aspect for the following year.

- *Which targets were selected?*

Gilbert Petit de Mirbeck: Companies who were Air Inter subscribers, companies requesting and receiving our time-tables on a regular basis, and companies with whom we had no contact. The first two targeted segments were given more weight in the test. Initial testing took place in July and the actual campaign was launched last September.

- *What results were obtained and how were they used?*

Gilbert Petit de Mirbeck: When a presentation was made, we found 54 per cent of calls resulted in interested clients for Air Inter.

Gérard Jouron: The information collected was then passed on to the different sales teams according to the geographic area and the importance of the detected potential, our lower limit having been set at 40 trips per year; we had decided not to arrange a visit below that limit. We are going to contact those prospects through other means.

Gilbert Petit de Mirbeck: That is where telemarketing has been effective: short-term results for the sales people and the possibility of setting up communication systems for on-going contacts with the other prospects on an on-going basis. This reflects the truth of the markets: all clients do not have the same level of needs and cannot be given the same level of sales effort.

● *What are your comments after this first experiment?*

Gérard Jouron: This type of operation often meets with reservations on the part of the sales force. They sometimes fear the company's image will be affected. In this case nothing of this kind was observed. The Air Inter brand is well-perceived. We are now researching means of developing our telephone operation. We are already very efficient in handling incoming calls because of our reservations centre. We now wish to develop outbound phoning.

Gilbert Petit de Mirbeck: Now we have proved the value of the method, we wish to develop the skills and applications by adapting various approaches and this will mean a change of structures and viewpoints.